D1067544

First Edition
1975

Published by
Trends Publishing Co.

Detroit, Mich. 48202

REMEMBRANCES OF THINGS PAST

by

Stanley H. Brams

Library of Congress
Catalog Card Number
75–21283

Printed in The Republic of China

PROLOGUE

A visitor sat in the office of Charles E. Wilson, president of General Motors in 1950. He watched with high interest while Wilson signed an approval for a new $250,000 airplane. Asked the visitor: "How many airplanes does General Motors have?"

Wilson replied, "I think about 15."

The visitor expressed surprise at the size of the fleet. Wilson ruminated a while. Then he remarked: "I guess the day has passed when a vice president is satisfied with a key to a private toilet."

I have long been in the newsgathering business, and I have brushed against many amusing and unusual situations. What follows are my (with apologies to Proust) remembrances of such things past—the kind of history that doesn't get into the record books.

REMEMBRANCES OF THINGS PAST

I began reporting when I was 14 years old, a junior at Bay City Central High School. I had been on publicity committees for various school activities and had become acquainted with the city editor of the Bay City Times Tribune, Joe Kerr. One day he said to me:

"Our school editor is leaving. How'd you like to do the Sunday school page, Stanley?"

I gulped. "How could I get around to all the schools?"

"You could use my car."

I nodded, struck dumb. He said: "I'll pay you six dollars a week."

And so, in late 1924, I became a reporter. It was a minor league training ground, but a tough one, too. My first summer found me doing general reporting, and I had my first abrasive lesson when I was sent to get some information from the head of a financial organization of some sort—perhaps a building and loan company. I returned and wrote the story.

Joe Kerr called me over. "What about such-and-such?"

I admitted I hadn't found out about such-and-such.

"Go back and get it," said Joe Kerr.

It was awkward indeed to intrude again on one who in my eyes was a major captain of commerce. But I did. I returned and wrote my new story.

Again Joe Kerr called me over. "What about so-and-so?"

I shook my head in desperation. "I didn't ask him."

"Go back and ask him."

I stood in the office building hallway, forlorn, afraid, and long minutes passed before I dared open the institution's door—me, then a 15-year-old annoying what in my eyes was a personage of great importance. Finally I steeled myself, went in, and got the information Joe Kerr insisted on.

As I write this, those happenings began a half-century ago. It has been a good career, a lucky career. I have traveled, enjoyed, savored—yes, and suffered, too, at times. This is a memory book for my sons, my friends and acquaintances, many named here, many familiar with the others around whom I have reminisced. Putting this together has stirred a happy string of memories of a quietly satisfying half-century. I hope it may provide some moments of pleasure, of amusement, maybe of nostalgia, for its readers.

Flurry for Fletcher

The export vice president of Chrysler, Irving J. Minett, and I moved from bar to bar in Atlanta one evening during the corporation preview there in 1968. On one of our very late stops, in a crowded room indeed, we saw Chrysler speech writer Jim Fletcher standing at the bar with someone else.

Minett nudged me. We moved behind Fletcher, a quiet man who took pride in his meticulous, well-rounded ghosting.

Said Minett: "You'd think these preview speeches would develop a new kind of routine, wouldn't you." It was just loud enough for Fletcher to hear. And he did hear—we could see his back arch a little bit and his head come subtly up, to be sure he wouldn't miss what was said behind him.

"Yes," I agreed, catching the cue. "Those speeches are always the same."

"Trouble is, they get duller every year," my companion went on. Fletcher's head began leaning almost grotesquely back.

I executed the coup de grace. "Even if they're dull," I said, "you'd think that whoever writes them would know enough to use good English."

Fletcher's pride was pricked beyond restraint. He turned around to face our burst of laughter.

Awkward Moments

The Detroit Free Press was beset by one of a series of periodic strikes in the sixties. Labor reporter Tom Nicholson wanted to go to an Auto Union convention in the east but lacked sponsorship—and an expense account. He borrowed an auto company car to save expenses and went anyway. Returning, he was driving the Ohio turnpike at extralegal speed and was overhauled by a traffic cop.

Nicholson, always resourceful, had a pathetic story to tell. "Officer," he said, "I work for the Free Press in Detroit. We've been on strike for two months. I'm out of money and I have kids at home—I've got to get a job. That's why I'm speeding—I don't have much time."

The officer was touched. He chided Nicholson and let him go.

Some weeks went by. Nicholson drove down to Pittsburgh to see his parents. One again he was returning on the Ohio Turnpike, this time at night—and once again he was speeding. A siren sounded behind him and a police car brought him to a stop. Nicholson waited, confident—he had his sad story ready, guaranteed to elicit sympathy.

The officer came alongside and shone a flashlight in Nicholson's face.

"Still looking for that job, eh?" said the state patrolman.

Nicholson for once was at a loss for words. He was taken to the nearest town, fined $25 and sent on his way—at reduced speed.

There was another UAW convention at Atlantic City during another strike. The then-labor reporter for The News, Jim Crellin, was bemoaning his confinement in Detroit to Leo Derderian, the proprietor of a favorite newsmen's hangout of that day, The Anchor Bar.

Leo was always accommodating. He said: "Why don't we both go?" He went to the safe, took out $400, and the two caught a midnight plane to Philadelphia, and there rented a car to Atlantic City. They touched the fringes of the convention for the next few days.

Walter Reuther had laid down an edict—no press conference till the convention ended. His aide, Joe Walsh, could do nothing about that, but as a publicity man he was distraught—he knew the press attendance would almost completely evaporate before the convention officially ended.

It did just that. On Saturday, the last day, the only ones there were I, having nothing to do till an appointment that evening in New York, a neophyte from one of the Philadelphia papers, and Crellin. Thin conference indeed for Reuther!

Leo Derderian was equipped with a pencil and pad. His presence at the 'conference' swelled the reportorial talent there by one-third. Reuther, a teetotaler, never knew he was facing perhaps the best known saloonkeeper in Detroit instead of a newsman.

He might have been embarrassed—for he did have the facility of embarrassment. I established that fact one day, walking through the General Motors building. There I spotted Reuther at the head of a small group which went into offices then there, of Paine, Webber, Jackson & Curtis—one of the larger firms of Wall Street against which Reuther inveighed so often.

I planted myself at the door and waited. Reuther came out. I confronted him: "What are you doing in a place like that?" I asked.

Reuther all but stuttered. "Why—why—these are a bunch of German trade unionists," he finally said. "I'm showing them around—I thought they ought to see how a broker operates."

That same building was the scene of an even more intense corporate embarrassment another time. Walking through during auto labor negotiations, I saw Chrysler's John Leary—Leary his company's topmost labor negotiating director—waiting for an express elevator, and this at a time when the companies were not admitting they had any contact whatsoever with each other during bargaining. I walked up to Leary.

"John, it's nice to see you," I said airily. Then I realized that he was accompanied by two other high officials, Lynn Townsend and John Riccardo, and bargaining team chief Bill O'Brien.

Leary flushed and swallowed. Townsend was more at ease and said hello. I beamed pleasantly and went my way. Leary, I learned later, had expressed deep worry when he arrived at the 14th floor and went in to talk with GM's Lou Seaton.

Writing (and Styling) Complications

General Motors Styling hired me in 1953 to write its life story. I spent a month with a tape recorder and division old-timers, hearing oral history—the only kind that existed. At the end I outlined the material, scoured the Bible till I found an apt title, "The Skilful Men," wrote a sample chapter and took it to the redoubtable Harley Earl—who could not draw a good line but knew instinctively what was valid and what could not succeed in the marketplace. Earl was an oddball among the standard auto executive types, eccentric and erratic, feared and respected, imperious, impulsive—and tremendously competent.

He liked what he saw. I spent six months, half-time, writing the book. A week went by after I handed in the manuscript, and then I got a phone call: "Mr. Earl doesn't like the book. Can you attend a dinner meeting at the Recess Club tomorrow night?" Of course I could.

Earl and his departmental and studio chiefs and I dined well. Then Earl pushed back his chair. "I read what this man wrote," he said. (I do not think he ever knew my name.) "It's not what I want. I blame my publications committee."

This was the first I knew there was a publications committee.

I said, "Mr. Earl—don't blame your people. They've given me every cooperation. I wrote simply what I thought you wanted—the way we talked about it."

He looked at me, seated at his right, and put his hand on my shoulder. "Look," he said, "I didn't come here to chastise anyone. But I have some prerogatives around here and I've simply decided I want it different."

He pulled a Chevrolet dry-as-dust history out of his pocket—a pamphlet that chronologically listed that division's achievements, year by year. "Leave out all those anecdotes and that kind of stuff," he said. "Just write the facts—like this."

He looked around the room. "Now I've got a meeting at the Grosse Point Yacht Club," he said. "You fellows work it out."

The door closed behind him. There was a moment of silence. Then the dozen men in the room began to roar so hard with laughter that they doubled up.

I had gotten to know them well, and I felt I had been spanked in public—and wrongly. ''What are all you sons of bitches laughing at?'' I asked.

The guffawing went on. ''Why,'' said one of them, ''you just found out how we design cars.''

Interview Trap

The general manager of GM's Pontiac division, Martin Caserio, presided at the customary Pontiac breakfast of the Chicago Auto Show in 1974 and took questions afterward.

Ward's Auto World's Dave Smith asked about cars of the future. "What will be the wheelbase of the 1980 car, Marty?" he wanted to know.

Caserio meditated, then mousetrapped his questioner. "You mean front wheel drive or rear wheel?" he asked.

Smith had visions of a revelation. He said, too casually, "Let's talk about front wheel drive."

Caserio beamed. "With front wheel drive," he said, "wheelbase doesn't matter."

Smith waved his white napkin over his head in total surrender.

High Stakes

Television photographer Murray Young and I began a gin rummy game on a Chrysler plane during World War II, heading for a plant dedication in Maryland. We continued the game in the motel after the dedication, and then again on the return plane ride. As we made our approach into City Airport in Detroit Young finally tallied the score of most of a day's gin playing, and found I was precisely one point ahead!

Said Young: "I'll tell you something. We haven't been playing for a fiftieth of a cent a point. We've been playing for a dollar a point. I never knew anybody who could afford to play gin for a dollar a point, and I'm going to pay you here and now and talk about it the rest of my life."

In front of the newsmen witnesses on the plane Murray paid off. And he did brag about it for some time to come.

The Previews

My first new car preview was at Indianwood Country Club, for the 1935 Plymouths. I will always remember a Casper Milquetoastish man with, yes, an umbrella, elderly John McMahon of the Daily Drovers Journal of Chicago. He took a fatherly kind of interest in this newcomer on the beat. Taking me aside he told me to beware of an uncouth character who, he said, was making trouble. This man had already loudly complained that the Club slot machines had been put there purposely to fleece the reporters; he had made such a scene that the publicity man for Plymouth, Bill Berchtold of the J. Stirling Getchell agency, had given him back $13.15 he claimed to have lost.

Sales manager Harry Moock of Plymouth presided at the dinner. He began what I was to learn was the standard preview speech of that era. ". . . We are glad to have you men with us, and we certainly appreciate the fine help you've given us this past year—and we hope our warm relationship continues through this coming year. . ." In the midst of these heartily delivered remarks the uncouth character stood up in the center of the horseshoe-shaped table arrangement and called out:

"Mister Chairmans, I vant to say few vords."

Moock, taken aback, hesitated, then said: "Well, of course—go ahead."

"Mister Chairmans, my name Harry Sogolowski. I publisher Dziennik Polski in Harrisburg—forty t'ousand circulation. All time I get da publicity from Plymout' company. I print it. Den I write Plymout' and say, 'I have run da publicity, now give me some advertising.' Dey never answer. I come Detroit and ask today for dis Harry Mooch who say all dese t'ings in da goddam publicity. Dey say he here. I try find him all time—can't."

He had worked his way up to where he stood across the table from Moock. "I vant say one t'ing to my fellow newspaper men," he shouted, "Da Plymout' company bring you all out here to take your money. Dey cheat just like da goddam publicity wid no advertising. Dis Harry Mooch is a thief. I tell him so if I ever—"

Moock was a peppery little man, an irascible Dutchman. He leaned far across the table and took a roundhouse swing at the Polish publisher. That worthy fell to the floor. His watch and chain sailed out of his vest across the room.

Sitting next to me was the grizzled Chris Sinsabaugh, editor of Automotive News. He jumped to his feet, shouting angrily. "You don't have to take that, Harry. Throw him out." Others were yelling, too. The cause of the commotion was somehow ushered out by waiters through the door leading to the kitchen.

Moock ran his hand through his hair. He straightened his coat and tie. "Gentlemen," he said. "I want to apologize for losing my temper. I don't know where that man came from—how he got here. He's not one of us. I'm sorry—I shouldn't have—"

Someone called from the kitchen door. "He wants to apologize."

Moock pondered a second. "Alright, let him in."

The disheveled publisher reappeared, walking slowly up into the horseshoe. "Chentlemens, I am so—I feel so bad. I no vanted make trouble. I just vanted tell—" and suddenly he straightened up and his voice surged out in renewed, bitter anger. "—tell how we all getting cheated by dis goddam Harry Mooch and his goddam publicity."

A circle of auto editors closed in on him. A voice rang out. "Hit the son of a bitch." Another: "Kick him outa here—hard."

It seemed that a gang beating was about to begin. But suddenly the circle opened up. The man was weeping, copiously, and the editors were nonplussed at the sight; they fell away.

Then there was an imperious rapping of a spoon on a glass. Moock was calling for order. "That's enough, you all," he cried.

Silence. Moock spoke quietly. "Gentlemen," he said, "I think it's time you got acquainted with my good friend from Pittsburgh, Luke Barnett."

The circle dissolved. The 'publisher' went around the table, up to Moock, and they shook hands before a suddenly silent audience.

Moock told how he had been made a laughingstock by Barnett the first time they met. And Barnett recounted some experiences—how Walter Chrysler had planted him as an usher at the Metropolitan Opera and how he had then ordered Mrs. Chrysler out of her box for talking too loudly—when she was one of the Met's largest supporters. How he had terrorized a hunting party of wealthy industrialists by letting them hear him hatch plans to blow up their lodge in revenge for some fancied slight—and so on. The auto editors were merely the latest in a long line of victims of Barnett's consummate artistry. A few, shamefacedly, admitted having been gulled before—and hadn't recognized their tormenter in a different characterization!

There have been endless previews since. The late thirties saw Buick stage an outdoor barbecue at Flint, served from glittering enormous copper pots—dealers and editors alike. Working into late morning at Detroit I missed that serving—fortunately. Best belief later was that the copper cleaner hadn't been quite wiped off. The diarrhea and vomiting that night gave the Statler Hotel plumbing in Detroit its worst workout.

The next morning it was Hupp's turn—that nameplate's last preview, as it turned out. I went to the Statler with my employer, Al Ward of Ward's Reports—who complained, walking over, of the unhappy night he had mysteriously suffered. At the hotel was a gallery of white, white faces. We heard agonized stories while the bus took us to the Grosse Pointe Yacht Club.

I drank a cocktail, then made my way to the men's room. One stall was occupied. A groan came from inside—then an anguished and fervent, "God damn Buick."

For a few years that preview was immortalized as the Buick Purge.

Buick was once the sponsor of a Hawaiian party preview. Waldo McNaught, then its publicist, had been to Honolulu and learned about sailor's grog. The result was a preview shambles—newsmen half-asleep by luncheon, somnolent and uncomprehending at the press conference afterward.

Ralph Watts of the Detroit News aroused from his literal grogginess to ask a question about the new models—a sensitive question, for Buicks were widely known as gas guzzlers.

"Ed, has Buick improved its fuel economy this year?"

Ragsdale, also somewhat the worse for alcoholic wear, straightened up pridefully.

"Buick," he proclaimed, "has always been a good friend of the oil companies."

Probably that was the most memorable preview statement of my experience. But there were others of major note.

Joe Bayne had gone from the sales managership of Chrysler-Plymouth to a similar post at Lincoln-Mercury and was presiding at his first press showing with his new company. He led his audience through a point-by-point review of the new Mercurys and the fundamental advances they embodied.

"In conclusion," he said, "I want to say just this—our new models are far and wide the best Plymouths we've ever built!" The snickers that followed left him bewildered, unknowing what he had said.

A Lincoln-Mercury general manager had an unhappier, more fundamentally amusing experience. Ben Mills ran that session in a day when many companies financed various types of auto racing—while simultaneously denying that they were thus violating the general tenets of industry policy.

In the midst of the preview press conference, under a tent at Ford's Sterling proving ground, northeast of Detroit, Ralph Watts again had a question on an awkward topic. He broke into a succession of sales outlook inquiries with a blunt and (to Mills) unhappy change of subject.

"Who pays Parnelli Jones?"

Mills played it cool. "I suppose he wins enough races to finance himself—he seems to win a lot of the time."

The question boomed out again in the suddenly quiet tent, where nearly everybody knew Jones drove Mercurys in stock car events.

"Who pays Parnelli Jones?"

"Why," said Mills, and the beginning of a fluster could be vaguely sensed in his hesitation. "Why. . .I don't know, I thought" (here he took a studied look around the bleacher seats before him) "—well, probably so-and-so could tell you, but I don't see him. I guess he isn't here."

An inept company aide tried to be helpful. "Mr. Mills, he's behind the tent," he called. "Should I get him?"

Mills looked dumbstruck at the man. "NEVER MIND," he shouted. The place shook with a roar of laughter.

There were the years of preview themes. An Olds circus—a main tent with the new cars, sideshows with their special features, popcorn, cotton candy—and of course plenty of food and drink. A Studebaker beach party with Uncle Sam suits for all (World War II had lately broken out in Europe).

Chevrolet had an elaborate musical performance in the late thirties of Ravel's "Bolero." The grand ballroom of Detroit's Statler Hotel was festooned with curtaining broken by vertical pillars. At each repetition of the Bolero theme one pillar split open to expose a husky black man, bare chested, wearing spangled tights and headdress, rhythmically striking a tympani with gold-wrapped mallets. As the music swelled more and more, other pillars opened; the tom-tom drumming increased, finally reaching a crescendo probably never duplicated before or since. Eardrums might have been punctured that night—but all were impressed nonetheless.

In that era Chevrolet would put the reporters' names in a hat to draw a winner of the Grand Prize of the evening—a new model Chevrolet. First came discussion of which drawee would win—would it be the initial name? the third? the seventh? The reportorial audience called out choices, settled on one. Some unhappy guests heard their names called too soon. The draw was surely honest—too often the winners were from obscure papers, and never from those which Chevrolet would have found purpose in blandishing.

Customarily after the draw Chevrolet's great sales manager, the late Bill Holler, would jump to his feet. "I'm going to donate another car," he would cry. "Draw another name." And they did.

Holler always grew great applause with his annual preview speech—a ritual statement. After a day of long, self-serving oratory, the reporters were deeply responsive to Holler's simple, sentence-long message:

"Boys, I have only one thing to say—keep a warm spot in your heart for Chevrolet!"

A Chevrolet new car was a lavish gift for someone, to be sure, but all were treated well in that period. Furniture, portable radios in a day when one radio console per household was standard, watches and other jewelry, clothing, cameras, kitchen utensil sets, electric power tools, glassware, shavers, even fancy shower heads, gift certificates—the tide of gifting ran high, a standard practice which everyone frowned on in principle but embraced in practice.

One year Chevrolet gave each man a piece of good luggage. A few days later the platoon of auto editors piled onto the Detroiter for the annual train ride to the National Automobile Show of prewar days in New York. At Grand Central destination the redcaps carried the luggage into the terminal and set it down—into the greatest suitcase confusion in history. Sixty or seventy identical bags in indiscriminate piles, few identifiable except by examination of contents!

The years after Korea saw the gift-giving continue, but in steadily smaller dimensions. Veteran preview goers, however, had by then accumulated large stores of identical miniature radios, trays, vases, cutlery, broilers, bowls, pewter pitchers and copper pots, clocks, other household apparati.

Len Barnes' wife loaned her cleaning woman to Hugh Quinn's household.

"My," said the cleaner to Donna Quinn, "this is just about like bein' at Mrs. Barnes—you got the same stuff!"

What the previews began to lack in big-ticket gifts, they made up in distance during one period. Ford's divisions ranged far and wide—one year at Flora, Ill., because it supposedly was American's population center, others all the way from San Diego to Cape Cod to Carefree, Ariz. Volkswagon took its guests to Nogales, Ariz., where one and all crossed the adjoining border into Mexico. General Motors divisions were mostly stay-at-homes, but Chevrolet did have two showings at Hidden Valley, near Gaylord, Mich., and another at a resort in northwestern Ohio.

Chrysler was the originator of the long-distance preview, and that company did the job lavishly—at least in its lavish income years. The first was at Miami Beach, at the Americana Hotel—two more followed there.

That was a time, now enforced only sketchily, of rigorous security on new model details. Chrysler had private guards at every entrance to the lobby. I went to the lower level coffee shop for breakfast one morning; when I returned to the circular staircase up to the lobby a guard stopped me—I had forgotten my badge.

Momentarily frustrated, I saw Chrysler's Jim Zeder approaching—one of the handful of men who ran the company. "He'll identify me," I told the guard.

"Where's his badge?" the guard wanted to know. Zeder also lacked his. We stood till someone came and vouched for both of us.

That was the preview when Ray Ellis of the Chicago Tribune proposed at 4 o'clock one morning that his group sign up for an option starting three hours later—a morning fishing trip. It was agreed to meet at the door. The bleary-eyed group assembled—all except Ellis. They rang his room.

"Fishing?" he mumbled. "You guys think I'm crazy? I just got to bed!"

The rest were up and dressed. They went fishing. They kept in their boat's live tank their smallest catch—a foot-long barracuda. The boatman yanked it out with tongs when they landed and wrapped it in newspaper and twine—tightly, for even baby barracudas have needle-sharp teeth. The group got a key to Ellis's room and spilled the barracuda into the toilet, barely in time for it to revive. There Ellis saw it snapping and thrashing when he returned to his room.

"There's a big fish in my toilet," he complained to the desk. The deskman presumably felt he was dealing with a drunk and his delusions, and paid him no heed for a considerable time.

It was at one of those Americana previews that Ed Hayes stumbled into an empty seat at the always-active poker game where John Rooney of the Boston Herald was a regular along with Charley Sievert of the late-lamented New York Telegram, me, and others of that earlier day. Of all us serious poker players, Rooney was by far the most serious—and one of the best.

Hayes, a poker tyro, and at that moment somewhat befuddled to boot, was a less than noteworthy addition to the game. He had to be told when it was his turn to bet, and he kept no track of the raises.

A hand of five-card stud was begun. With the second exposed card dealt Rooney had two jacks showing. He bet the limit, $2—a big bet for that day. Everyone dropped out except Hayes, who had showing a two of spades and eight of hearts. Another card was dealt—Rooney hadn't visibly improved, and Hayes got a queen. Again Rooney bet $2; again Hayes called. On the fifth card Hayes got a second queen, and Rooney disgustedly threw in his hand. He glared at Hayes, who was vaguely gathering in the pot, then reached across and turned up his opponent's hole card.

It was a nine of diamonds. Hayes had met Rooney's paired jacks with three lower cards which did not match any way at all. Rooney rose in thunderous wrath, pointed his finger at Hayes, and bellowed:

"Out of the game! Get out of the game, you— you—!"

Hayes shoveled his winnings into his pocket and left.

Not all games had such amusing moments. For some years one auto editor who often played had some disquieting habits. He would put a five-dollar bill into the pot and take change for a ten. Or he would play light by withdrawing some money, then he would bet as if it were his own. We all saw those peccadilloes, but none had the heart to call the miscreant. Jim Jones of Newsweek finally did.

"We're all tired of the way you keep shortchanging the pot," he snapped. "Now you just put in a ten and took nineteen dollars out. Put it back, and you better get out of the game."

A piteous look came over the man. "I can't help it," he said haltingly. He never played again.

The Chrysler long distance previews branched out from Miami and covered the nation. The company sought out brand-new hotels in centers where wire and phone facilities were adequate for the thousands upon thousands of words the newsmen would send out. By then the select 50 or 75 print editors of the forties had been amplified by radio and television reporters, and a respectable preview might attract (at company expense) as many as 200 or more newsmen. Chrysler took whole hotels or major shares of them for three-day stands in Boston, Los Angeles, Dallas, Pittsburgh, Kansas City, elsewhere.

At Dallas, a publisher broke the unwritten rule and smuggled his wife into the preview hotel. All rooms were double, so there was no physical problem. Her own comings and goings created no difficulty; Chrysler had only half that hotel's rooms.

The second night saw the publisher drink overlong, and he finally fell off his bar stool. Others tugged and hauled him to his room. There his wife's key was in the lock inside, and she—following his instruction to open the door only when he knocked in a certain way and not to answer the telephone—did not remove it. The would-be helpers of the besotted publisher were unable to get the key they had taken from his pocket fully into the lock. The confusion was finally resolved—but the publisher never appeared at another Chrysler preview.

Ford had a showing of another sort—of its desert proving grounds, at Kingman, Ariz., in February of 1956. A radio man from Los Angeles proved particularly obnoxious to the Detroit veterans. He capped his misbehavings by elbowing his way into the ever-present poker game, slapping down on the table an ancient pistol and announcing that "from now on it will be an honest game."

Jim Jones, irked, possessed himself of the weapon. The radio man grabbed for it and Jim tossed it across the room to someone else. Like a child chasing in a game of catch, the radio man ran, trying to intercept the now-continually-tossed pistol. Finally the inevitable—someone dropped it, and a large chunk of the old casting broke off.

The Los Angeleno blamed Jones and, in character, squeaked. "I just paid $30 for that antique and now you've busted it. I know Hank Ford Junior and I'm going to get your job!"

Jones assumed supplication in the public relations role mistakenly thrust upon him. "Oh, please don't," he pleaded. "Here we bring you fellows in to make friends and this happens!" He pulled out his wallet and half-whispered, "will five dollars square it?"

"Don't try to bribe me," cried the radio man. It is not of record that he ever reached Hank Ford Junior—whom nobody ever called Hank Junior.

It was at this event that Jones felt an overwhelming urge to go to nearby Las Vegas and its dice tables. We tried to borrow a car, but the canny Ford publicists feared we would never return for Ernie Breech's dedication ceremony the next day. Disgusted, Jones—at 3 o'clock in the morning—called Charles Moore, Ford's public relations vice president, and woke him from a sound sleep.

"I want to borrow a car down here at Kingman," Jones said. "I can't get one."

To a half-awake ear the complaint sounded valid. "Ask one of my guys—Hefty or Murphy or someone."

"Your guys," Jones told him, "have all disappeared. Haven't seen one of them for three or four hours."

It is said there was an angry telephone confrontation the next morning, dispelled only when the luckless publicists at Kingman convinced their boss that Jones was playing games, and that right was on their side.

It was at this preview that publicist Marc Parsons had a hand in what was to be a surprise. A Ford vehicle was to run an obstacle course around a set of barrels, then finally knock all the barrels over—and out from under each one would come streaking a desert hare, cached there beforehand. The event came off, but it was after a long period of hot sunshine. The rabbits were too heat-stricken to streak away—they simply sat, and youngsters from the vicinity, there to take a hand in the proceedings, ran up, grabbed and made off with them.

Nash Motors and its successor companies had previews for a long succession of years in Wisconsin—at Brown's Landing, at Lake Geneva, and points in between. I was unable to go one year in the late thirties, and a few days later I met the then-auto editor of the Detroit News, E. Y. Watson. Watson was a profane, sickly, cranky man who usually wore an overcoat, summer or winter, to warm up his thin blood. I asked him about the preview.

"It was awful," he half-grunted, half-whined—his typical voice. "We got to some place in Wisconsin and they put us on a goddam boat. We went across some goddam lake and the goddam wind was blowing something awful. I was never so goddam cold in my life. Why do those goddam fools have a preview in such a goddam place?"

A decade or so later I drove out of Brown's Landing with a lady publicist for Nash-Kelvinator from Chicago. We had decided to go dancing. In Kenosha we ran into utter disbelief—a girl hotel clerk. Answering my inquiry whether they had a supper room for dancing, she said with a sneer: "Well, I guess we could roll up the rug and turn up the Muzak—but that's all."

We drove down the street. My friend, a cheery type, stopped at a light and hailed a stranger: "Say, is there any place around here we could go dancing?"

"Dancing? Why waste your time dancing? If you want to go to bed, you can drive out the highway and any motel'll take you in, whether you're married or not. You don't need luggage."

My friend replied sweetly: "We are married, but it happens we're married to different people."

"Well," said the man, "you can go to the hotel back there if you don't want to waste time getting out to the highway."

Said my friend: "Say, you're more entertaining than anything we have at Brown's Landing? Maybe you'd better come back there with us."

"What you doing at Brown's Landing?"

"We're at a Nash-Kelvinator preview."

"Nash?—Nash has ruined this town. I know—I'm a city councilman."

"How do you mean?" she asked.

"Why, Nash brought a lot of hillbillies up from the South, and they got all our girls pregnant."

"I thought," said my friend, "that it took two to do that."

After some further conversation we drove off.

During one of its lean periods Chrysler portaged the press on a local cruise boat to Cleveland. We went aboard between two columns of bagpipers and drummers—the company at that time supported a Scottish band.

As our car drove up the gangplank, war veteran Grant Howell, the editor of Royal Oak's Tribune, turned to me. "The last time I was piped aboard a boat," he said, "I didn't get back for four years."

More entertaining than that preview or many others were the annual Volkswagen showings. Having nothing of styling or mechanical note to talk about during the years VW stayed almost identical, the company's vice president, Art Railton, produced parodies on major introductions—long dissertations on an added quarter-inch of glass all around, or on the slightly enlarged gasoline tank caps. His humor was superb. Everyone has always felt VW previews produce completely unadulterated enjoyment.

Fuel Economy Formula

Tom Kleene's name is often pronounced 'clean' by strangers, but often his remarks don't quite live up to that adjective. We often paired together in what was for a time an annual Volkswagen preview feature—a road rally. Kleene and I won several years running until one confused year when we went badly off course, passed a church four times trying to find our way back onto course, and finally arrived so late that an extra prize and a suitable one was arranged for each of us—a fat ham.

But Kleene's immortality in those affairs was assured the year we won the prize for economy. Asked how we could possibly have used so little fuel, Tom thoughtfully replied, "Brams urinated in the gas tank."

(It was Kleene, fairly recently, who recalled to me the moment when we played one hole of golf at a Pontiac preview with Jack Nicklaus. Nicklaus watched me loft a ball a bit off course—and a bit short. Said he: "Stanley, we've got to do something about your swing.")

Accessory?

The Bronco was a Ford open platform vehicle patterned somewhat after the Jeep and the Mutt—a truck-like unit with some passenger car amenities. At its introduction a reporter asked Ford general manager Donald Frey if air conditioning would be available. "Yes," Frey replied, "we have a model without any doors."

Negotiation Backfire

Profanity and obscenity are often hallmarks of private labor negotiations, much of it intentional, aimed at upsetting the aplomb—and judgment—of the man on the other side of the table. For strategic reasons and often because of genuine temper, the late president of the Intl. Electrical Union, Jim Carey, was known far and wide as a master of obscenity.

During one negotiation the head of the General Motors bargaining team, Heinie Gierok, walked out of a meeting with Carey and his people, saying he wouldn't stand for the kind of language he was hearing.

I went to New York some days later, where Carey and other IUE negotiators were then meeting with General Electric. I stopped in to ask the head of the General Electric negotiations, Virgil Day, if he could tell me anything of what was happening. Day came out of the negotiations and we talked for a time. Then he said:

"Does Carey know you?"

I said he did.

Said Day: "Too bad. He is going in great form today. If he didn't know you, I'd have you drop in and sit in a corner like a staff man—you'd be fascinated by the way he's carrying on."

I expressed real regrets. Day went on, with a smile. "Oh, say, I have a message for your General Motors friends. Tell them if they expect to negotiate with Jim Carey they'd better get some callouses on their skins, so they won't feel the need of walking out of a negotiation."

I promised to deliver the message. I got on the Detroiter that night and settled back in my berth to read the late edition papers I had bought before boarding. One of them had a small boxed item on the front page:

"Virgil Day and his General Electric negotiators walked out of their meeting today with Intl. Electrical Union bargainers. Day said he did not have to stand for the kind of language Carey was using and the insults he was delivering."

Carey's Commotion

Jim Carey had the facility of quick anger over any disagreement. I attended the Milwaukee convention of his Intl. Electrical Union at which the constitution of the then-new organization was to be adopted.

It was a dull meeting indeed—paragraph after paragraph of legal language, discussion, passage. Near the end of two days of this, the committee chairman began to read a clause saying that the annual convention would be held annually during the latter half of November.

A delegate rose, "Why do we have to have a convention in weather like this?" he inquired plaintively. "My partner is back at the hotel in bed. I think he's got pneumonia from sloshing around in all this snow and wet and raw weather."

Carey undertook to answer. "The committee considered this very carefully," he said. "We have to have our convention at a time before our big negotiations with General Electric and Westinghouse. This is the best time to have it."

The delegate persisted. "All the same," he said, "there ought to be a better time. I'll bet it's 28 degrees outside."

Said Carey: "You're wrong. It's 33 or 34."

Voices rose from the floor—the first opportunity for an issue, however small, since the reading of the constitution had begun the day before.

"It's 28," the cries rang out. "It's 26. . . . You're wrong, Carey."

Carey pounded the gavel. "It's 34," he shouted.

The voices rose above the pounding of the gavel. The convention dissolved in uproar over how cold it was outside. Carey, never a diplomat, suffused by his own anger, couldn't gavel down the commotion. It ended only when he adjourned the session.

Bad-Man Boulware

Jim Carey's most publicized opponent in his earlier days of IUE leadership was the redoubtable Lem Boulware of General Electric. Boulware, by his frank admission, was completely expendable if he made a mistake. He enjoyed the kind of raw-boned battling he said characterized labor relations—and the hard reputation he had for doing it. His bargaining weapons, so to speak, were generally far stronger than Carey's for a variety of reasons. He emerged from one negotiation with an especially successful contract from management's standpoint.

Tex Colbert, then president of Chrysler, asked me who had been responsible for such a resounding victory. I told him.

Later I ran into Boulware and remarked on Colbert's compliment. Said he:

"If people begin to say good things about me, I'm getting out of character. I must be slipping!"

A Horse on Nute

Al Nute left his business news editorship of the Toledo Blade to become public relations manager for Graham-Paige at Detroit. The then-treasurer of that company, W. L. Eaton, had hired him. Eaton had the reputation of being a hard and sarcastic man, and his elderly crustiness was amplified by the fact that he wore a hearing aid—and ostentatiously turned it off when anyone dared to talk back to him. He and Nute soon were at sharp odds but Nute, having quit a secure berth in Toledo, saw no choice but to live with his problems.

One day, walking down the executive corridor, he passed Eaton's office and was summoned in. "Sit down, Mr. Nute," said Eaton with a thin smile.

Nute sat down. Eaton began to talk. "I don't know that you are familiar with my background, Mr. Nute. Before I came here I was the biggest distributor Graham-Paige had—I ran the whole west coast. And besides that, I had a fine stable—I was known as one of the leading horsemen of the West.

"One day," he went on, "I was up in Vancouver and I ran into an acquaintance. He told me he had a horse which he thought would interest me. I went out to look at the animal. She was a beautiful horse—well marked, nicely gaited. I resolved I would pay as much as twelve hundred dollars for her."

Nute sat back, listening to this pleasant recital. The thought went through his mind that finally he had cracked the old man's tough hide—he was on a reminiscence basis with him. Eaton continued:

"The man said to me, 'what will you give me for her?' I said I never put a price on another man's property—what did he want for her? He said eight hundred dollars. I said, 'sold,' and wrote him a check and gave instructions how the horse was to be shipped.

"I went on my way and got back home about ten days later. After a time I walked down to the stable, and my groom met me there. He told me the horse had arrived from Vancouver."

Eaton paused. "He said to me, 'how much did you pay for that horse, Mr. Eaton?' I didn't want to tell him that ridiculous price I had paid, so I said a thousand dollars.

"'Mr. Eaton,' my groom said, 'did you look that horse over thoroughly before you bought her?' I said I thought I had.

"'Well, Mr. Eaton,' he said, 'I'm sorry to have to tell you that the horse is blind in one eye and will be blind before too long in the other.'"

Eaton sat back in his chair and beamed. "Mr. Nute," he said, "I suppose you wonder why I tell you this story."

Nute beamed back and nodded his head.

"I'll tell you, Mr. Nute." And suddenly the voice became loud and angry. "I'll tell you, Mr. Nute—I was blind when I hired you! I was blind when I hired you!"

Homes Away from Home

For many years I have spent 90 to 100 days a year traveling, living in hotels. Ten years of this equal 900 days. Three years or so in hotel rooms! When I leave one I look back and think, "Here, once more, I have left a small bit of my life."

The grandest room was at the Shamrock, in Houston—a suite, actually, with giant reception room, kitchen, three clothes closets, bedroom, dressing room, enormous bath, two color televisions, all for about $14 a night in 1972! I had apparently been the last to arrive in Houston with a confirmed reservation for an Intl. Electrical Union convention—and not a regular room left. There were but six such suites on the entire floor.

Equally large, but threadbare, was the Presidential Suite at the Hollenden in Cleveland in the fifties, before its rebuilding. By mischance I had been billeted for an Auto Union convention halfway to Akron, in a lodging charitably called a hotel, best characterized by my having to leave a 50-cent deposit for a room key. I had protested routinely when I was so assigned, but when I saw the place my anger mounted. UAW's Frank Winn sent an aide with me to the union housing director. That harassed man, a line of problems in front of him, screamed angrily: "I'm no goddammed carpenter. I can't make rooms! I got no more rooms!"

The aide spread his hands helplessly. We retreated. I laid in wait for Winn. In a few minutes he came by.

"I thought you had influence in this union," I said bitingly. "You're just an errand boy I guess."

Winn whitened. "You still have no room downtown?" "No," I spat out.

"Wait here."

He disappeared. Ten minutes later he returned. "Go to Parlor B and a man will deliver you a key," he said.

My anger melted. Frank, after all, was my friend. I thanked him and went to Parlor B—a narrow room with a long table running its length.

Presently the housing director came in. He glared at me.

"Here's your room," he snarled. He slammed a key on the table and it skittered down to me at its end. "That's the Presidential Suite," he yelled. "Only Walter Reuther could have made me give it up. If Estes Kefauver comes in tonight, God knows what I'll do with him—sleep him on a fire escape. You've made me more trouble than any other guy at this convention. I hope there are bugs in your bed. I hope the termites in the wall keep you awake all night." He slammed the door shut behind him.

That night we set up a poker game in an anteroom of the giant suite. The overhead light wouldn't turn on. "Call the housing guy," one of my poker friends suggested. "Tell him you're not satisfied with the room!"

As I pass through towns again and again I remember hotels, rooms, circumstances.

New York—an endless chain. The Drake, where we flew in for a foreign car showing, started a poker game, went around the corner to the showing, returned to the poker, played the rest of the night before flying back in the morning, having never left the place except for the short trip to see the new car.

The Waldorf, over and over again for Motoramas of the fifties. It was there that I ran into Lenore Romney, unhappy that her George was making his first major speech—and because it was before a men-only audience, she couldn't hear him. Thanks to Motoramas, I knew back stairs to the grand ballroom balcony. We sat inconspicuously at the rear of a box while George spoke.

The chain of memories. There was another back route to another ballroom, at the Plaza, in my college days. Thanks to it I attended a Columbia Junior Prom sans ticket.

Atlantic City. At a Steel Worker convention in late 1974 I met Archie Robinson of U. S. News on the boardwalk. "I was taking a nostalgic walk past the Ambassador—it's all boarded up," he said. It was at the Ambassador where endless union conventions headquartered in the forties and fifties before other cities built adequate facilities for big meetings.

The Chelsea was in those days next door to the Ambassador, an ancient wooden pile. (Said Archie Robinson: "I always asked at the Ambassador for a room away from the Chelsea side. I didn't want to wake up and see the place a sheet of flame one night.")

It didn't burn. I passed it one day and saw it advertised for sale that very morning—courtesy of the U. S. Referee in Bankruptcy. I went in. The place was bare save for a small crowd of men—30 or 40—in the ballroom. Two were sitting directly in front of me on a kitchen table, the only remaining furniture. Bidding began. The auctioneer started at $250,000, and went up in $50,000 steps. At $450,000 the one man on the kitchen table momentarily stopped his conversation and nodded at the auctioneer, who intoned, "I now have five hundred." At five-fifty the man on the table interrupted his conversation again to nod once more—and then he resumed talking. He repeated this at a level of six hundred and fifty thousand, but then, when the auctioneer sought his bid after seven hundred and fifty thousand, he shook his head no—and went back to his conversation.

I was impressed by such nonchalance. Then, the next day, I was completely perplexed to see him walking down the aisle of the Steel Worker convention I was covering. I stopped him and introduced myself.

"You must pardon my curiosity," I said. "I saw you bid nearly three quarters of a million dollars yesterday for the Chelsea—and now I see you at a union convention. Those pieces just don't fit. How does this happen?"

"Very simple," he said. "My name's Lawrence Tisch. I'm in the hotel business. I do a lot of business with unions—that's why I'm here."

Later, many times later, I saw Tisch at the Americana in Miami Beach—it was then his property..

I went to the Americana for the first time a few weeks after it opened, at a Chrysler preview. There, during a later preview, Hurricane Donna, one of the worst, imprisoned us for two days.

The city editor of the Detroit News came to me as this blow was nearing its climax. "I've asked Ralph Watts to write me a piece on Detroiters in a hurricane and he refused—said that wasn't his beat. How'd you like to do it?—for money?"

The chance to write general spot news—especially news that could be whipped up dramatically—was compelling, money or no. I wrote the piece; it ran on Page One of the News. My friend, Watts, the News auto editor, read it in a pensive moment and momentarily feared I was trying to get his job. He was somewhat cool to me for a time.

More amusing was another hotel incident involving Ralph. We were all at the Waldorf, at one of those New York Motoramas. Late at night in someone's room we felt Ralph's presence would add a happy note. We phoned him just as he was getting into bed. He promised to join us at once.

Ten minutes went by. Then—a hurried, worried rapping on the door. We let Ralph in—slippered, wearing only pajamas whose brilliant red would have paled any fire engine. He had a lurid story. Walking toward the elevator he had scared someone—a house detective had chased him—he had fled from floor to floor by stairwell and elevator. True? False? We never knew. But we enjoyed the story.

Such ghosts of memories! All the way from the Chevron in Melbourne, Australia, to the Malmer in Stockholm. At the Grand Tahiti in Papeete I checked in the day after Raymond Burr, famed as the defense attorney, Perry Mason, and later as Chief Ironsides, had checked out. Who was with Burr? Naturally enough, his rival of his television court appearances, the prosecutor who never won a case, William Talman, who played Hamilton Burger.

It was at that hotel, too, that I began to talk to a young man fishing from the pier, and found out that he was a Columbia scholarship winner from Oak Park—one of the people I had helped gain admission to my college!

At Detroit's Tuller one bitterly cold night a fire aroused guests. It was mostly smoke, but many were removed down firemen's ladders—among them a fairly elderly couple.

Hank Shurmur, a get-the-story-at-any-cost television cameraman for WWJ-TV, had arrived at the scene. He met the couple at the foot of the ladder. "Stay right there," he ordered. A meticulous workman, he held one end of a long tape measure to the nose of a man while an assistant unrolled it back to the camera to fix the focus. Shurmur walked to the camera.

The shivering couple, robes over nightclothes in the bitter air, turned uncertainly toward the hotel door. Shurmur whirled around.

"Goddammit," he bellowed. "Don't you move! Stay where you are, dammit!" Coarsely, imperious, Shurmur brooked no obstacle, no objection. His victims were intimidated. They stood still long enough for Shurmur to get his footage. It is not of record whether they died the next day of pneumonia.

The first foreign hotel to enter my consciousness came in my early days of auto industry reporting. A company function of some sort saw me seated at a table with C. B. Thomas, then export vice-president of Chrysler, and George Slocum, publisher then of Automotive News. Thomas had just returned from Europe and he remarked that he had stayed at the George V in Paris. "Ah," said Slocum tenderly—showing off his savoir faire. "How is the George V?" "It's as fine as ever, George." "Ah, the wonderful George V," murmured Slocum.

I noted that they pronounced the "V" perfectly—'senk'. But the rolling French "G" was beyond either of them.

Many years later, on my first trip to Spain's South Coast, I came off a plane at Malaga and saw a familiar name—"Jorge V". Taking a chance that it might be nearly as good in Torremolinos as its namesake in Paris, I spent my first night on the Costa del Sol there.

The world abroad has many hotels, superb to mediocre. The great ones—Hong Kong's Mandarin (I now buy its soap for special showoff for my guest bathroom); the Ritz in Lisbon and again in Madrid, the Inn on the Park and lately the Athenaeum in London and the Churchill as well (the manager there rings you up after you register to inquire if all is to your satisfaction); the El Minzah in Tangier; the Rabat Hilton (I tried the coffee shop there the morning of an early departure and found it dark—turned and confronted the dining manager, moving rapidly in his long Arabic skirt, almost wailing to me, "they are making a strike!")

And others. A room above a tiny restaurant in Agadir, Morocco—the only one left in a town where I came, ignorantly, without reservation. (As I departed two days later an English youth stopped me. "Do they have a room?—I slept in my car last night." I told him I was leaving; maybe my room was available. But Madam Manager came up, firmly said, "Eet is reserved—I am sorry.")

At the High Cliff in Bournemouth, on the English Channel ("PLEASE read the Fire Notice on display"), the upper halves of the windows were pulled down by rope pulleys, one on each side—my first acquaintance with that English standard.

At the Tivoli in Lisbon I couldn't sleep on a departure night, having drunk too much expresso at dinner. I read everything in sight, then put 10 escudos in the machine supposed to provide a "soothing, relaxing message in bed." No response. The next morning as I checked out I suggested I had a 10-escudo credit due, and explained why.

"Those are not our machines," said the cashier coldly.

The man behind me cut in. "I put 10 escudos in mine and blew out all my lights!"

"Did you call the floor maid?" the cashier asked me.

I said no, it was one o'clock in the morning. He said I should have called her. I paid my bill and went up to get my belongings. The two floor maids were in front of my door. I called them and in pantomine—I have no Portuguese—I explained what had happened. The one maid picked up the coin box, heavy with escudos, and banged it vigorously on the table. The bed began to undulate gently. I gathered my bags and left for the airport.

The 1965 AFL-CIO convention in San Francisco moved in to the Fairmont Hotel on the heels of Nikita Khruschev and his entourage—in fact, the two groups overlapped for a day or so.

The Russian contingent had the entire eleventh floor of the hotel. On their last day, while the AFL-CIO hierarchy was already fairly well ensconced, one laborite came excitedly in from the street. He saw a familiar face, the well known Washington labor priest, Msgr. George Higgins.

"Father," he panted, "there's smoke coming from a window on Khruschev's floor."

It was natural for the calm prelate to think of the process of voting for a Pope. "Was it white smoke or black smoke?" he inquired.

It was this same Fr. Higgins, many years earlier, at a UAW convention in Cleveland, who broke in on a conversation between labor columnist Vic Riesel and the labor editor of the Daily Worker, George Morris.

"George," said Riesel, "I think I'm going to write a column and say you're the most knowledgeable labor writer in the country."

"Vic," interjected Fr. Higgins, in the same joking vein, "if you write something like that I'll excommunicate you."

"Father," retorted Riesel, "I'm not in your jurisdiction!"

A Pre-Nixon Taping

Ben Gunner, as plant protection chief for Chrysler Corp., had a habit of talking like a movie tough—out of the corner of his mouth, confidentially. Whatever he said, no matter how minor, was apt to be delivered in this conspiratorial fashion.

One day he came into the office of B. E. Hutchinson, the hard-boiled vice chairman of the board and the financial man of the company, with some information to impart. He sat down and began to report his tidings in a low, confidential voice, delivered from the corner of his mouth. Hutchinson listened carefully, and kept craning his head forward. "What did you say, Ben?" he asked several times, motioning him closer and closer. Gunner was leaning well across the desk before he finished. He wound up his report with this admonition. "You have to be careful who you tell things like that to."

"You're right, Ben," Hutchinson agreed. "And you have to be careful where you tell them, too."

With that he flipped a switch and a record began to play back the conversation. Hutchinson, a cunning man, had enticed Gunner into talking over an ashtray which contained a hidden microphone.

Flushed and angry, Gunner stood up. "God damn you," he said, and stalked from the room.

No Credit

I cannot vouch for this story. I was not there. But it was told to me how Universal Credit Co., a Ford subsidiary, linked up with C.I.T. instead of Commercial Credit, the originally intended partner.

Commercial Credit's chairman, one Mr. Duncan, I was told, came to Dearborn to close the deal with the original Henry Ford. His appointment was on a Sunday morning, and the choice of that day—he being a good Scotch Presbyterian—offended him somewhat. His feelings were further rankled when Mr. Ford was late. The elder Ford had gone walking on his estate and had forgotten the appointment.

He bounded in finally and apologized profusely. They began small talk.

"You're from Baltimore, I understand, Mr. Duncan."

"Yes, Mr. Ford."

The auto man meditated. "I think of Baltimore in an unusual way," he said. "Baltimore was the site of the last shot tower in the United States."

The Commercial Credit man knew what was being talked about—a tower of colonial days from which molten lead was dropped in small globules which rounded out in their descent, then were quenched in a barrel on the ground and thus became cannon shot.

"There was a shot tower in Baltimore," he said. "But it was not the last shot tower in the country, Mr. Ford. The last shot tower was in Tunkhannock, Pa., where I was born."

"Oh, no," said Mr. Ford. "I had my scouts for Greenfield Village search the country over, and they told me Baltimore was where the last one was."

"I'm sorry to contradict you, Mr. Ford, but the last shot tower was in Tunkhannock."

"It was in Baltimore, Mr. Duncan."

"I say it was in Tunkhannock, Mr. Ford."

Ford rose angrily. "Mr. Duncan," he said, "the meeting is over."

And Universal Credit merged with C.I.T.

More Than You Promise

Paul Hoffman first came to Studebaker's attention when he won a contest in 1914 on "how to sell Studebakers". The prize of the contest was a personal interview with J. M. Studebaker—no more, no less. He went in to talk to the elderly founder of the company, then well along in his seventies. The founder was carefully slitting envelopes. He remarked, "The people downstairs buy scratchpads. I don't think that's necessary—I can use these envelopes."

Hoffmen knew that Studebaker was frugal—the evidence was in the fact that an interview was his only prize for emerging victorious in the contest.

Studebaker talked about this and that, then he said: "Young man, I will tell you how to be a success in business. Always give them more than you promise." He paused. "But don't give them too much more," he admonished, "or you'll go broke."

A Sampler for Selling

One of the first cars ever sold by Paul Hoffman was a second hand Jackson touring car, back about 1910 in Chicago. The prospect agreed to buy it if Hoffman could drive the car from Chicago to his home in St. Charles, about 35 miles away. Hoffman took the chance and made the distance; later he and the prospect went to the kitchen to close the deal.

The prospect had $500 for the car in his hand. He looked Hoffman squarely in the eye and said, "Young man, if you were in my place would you buy this car?"

Uncomfortable, Hoffman wriggled and his eye strayed. It lit on the opposite wall, where a sampler was done in bright colored yarns. Its message was "Jesus Hears Every Word You Say".

Hoffman gulped and answered, finally, "No, sir, I wouldn't but I haven't got $500. If I had $500 I wouldn't know where to get a better car for the money."

Hoffman's ecclesiastical standing was maintained—and he closed the deal.

Human Frailty

In 1951 the Public Relations Society of America held one of its annual banquets at the Waldorf-Astoria in New York City. Timewise, it was a disaster.

The cocktail hour ran overlong. The service was slow. When the first of a series of honored guests was introduced, he replied, not with a wave of his hand, but with a few minutes of observations. Thereupon the others did the same.

The hands of the clock had reached 11:30 when the main speaker was introduced. He indicated he had some remarks to make, even if the hour was late, and he went into them. The PRSA members filed out at midnight.

The next day Tony DeLorenzo was on his way home in a GM plane with Charles Kettering. Tony told Boss Ket about the evening before.

"Imagine!" he said. "These people are the arrangers—the fixers—the people who are supposed to have things run smooth. And they had a debacle like that!"

The Boss leaned back, closed his eyes and meditated. Then he opened them.

"Young man," he said, "only when you get to be as old as I am will you realize how stupid people can be."

Talking With People

My first Important Interviewee was the president of the New York Central Railroad. I was 20, between terms at Columbia College of Columbia University, the publicist and semi-manager of the Eastern Michigan Water Carnival. Coming into Cheboygan to arrange for selection of a Miss Cheboygan for the Carnival, a desk clerk told me:

"You know something? The President of the New York Central, Pat Crowley, was here today!"

"Where is he now?"

"Gone to Mackinaw City, I heard."

I hastened to the railroad depot. Sure enough, Patrick Crowley's private car had gone to Mackinaw City and would be on a siding there overnight. I left an early call and started northward shortly after 6 a.m.

In the yards at Mackinaw City on a sidetrack sat a sleeper of sorts, labeled No. 1. Now, for the first time, I was indecisive, irresolute, unsure. But I swung up the steps and found myself in a corridor with a blind turn ahead. A porter came around the turn.

"Do you want something?"

"I want to see Mr. Crowley. I'm a reporter."

The man disappeared. I heard him say, "There's a reporter wants to see you, Mr. Crowley." And a voice: "Send him in."

I followed the porter into a room where four men sat around a breakfast table. One, smallish, with the bushiest brows I had ever seen, held out his hand.

"I'm Patrick Crowley."

I told him my name, "—a reporter from the Bay City Times Tribune." He introduced me to the others—Henry Shearer, the general manager of the Michigan Central, an official named Starbuck, and another whose name has now left me.

"Have you had breakfast, Mr. Brams?"

I lied and said I had. "Maybe you'd have a cup of coffee with us," said Crowley. He ordered a place set, and beckoned me to sit down.

"Now, Mr. Brams, what would you like to interview me about?"

I was suddenly at a loss. I had not thought that far. I remember that I recovered and what I said—maybe inelegantly:

"Whatever you'd like to talk about, sir—business and how long this depression will last, or what you think of Michigan and how it looks to you—or whatever you'd like."

Crowley pondered. "Let me tell you about this morning. I got up about six and walked down to the docks. There was a young boy there, fishing with a line and bent pin. I borrowed it and tried for a few minutes—but I didn't get anything."

Shearer interjected. "Mr. Crowley isn't really much of a fisherman," he joked.

A few casual minutes followed. "Now," said Crowley, "I have to inspect the yards. Want to come along?"

I tagged along beside him to the stationmaster's. He called for the books and flipped through them—knowingly. We walked the rails, he studying the ties, the gravel, the joints. He talked about routine maintenance, and we ended back at Car No. 1.

There he said goodbye. I walked to my car on air—this was a quantum leap beyond asking the federal court clerk in Bay City what new cases had been filed. And, far more, I was touched deeply by the grave courtesy of a tycoon to a (and I knew) flustered, unsure, immature small town paper reporter.

One lesson I learned. The big people—in spirit and character more than in status—are considerate people. It is the little ones who, having risen to important places, are aloof and difficult—hiding their inadequacies, I assume.

As the years went on the brushes with Important Figures increased. Naturally I came to know any number of automotive executives on a first name basis, and any number of labor leaders. Some politicians, too.

In the early fifties, having left McGraw-Hill, I talked to Henry Ford II about an automotive magazine I proposed to publish. I told him I wanted no money of his—nothing of what became known later as a conflict of interest—but I did want suggestions as to where I might raise the quarter of a million dollars I estimated I would need.

"Try Laurance Rockefeller," Ford said. "He's gotten into some publishing ventures lately."

I wrote Rockefeller. Back came a letter from his secretary, whose name is now lost in my memory, but whom I will call Mrs. Smith. Mr. Rockefeller, she wrote, was in Europe and would still be there when I was to arrive in New York.

I waited till my next trip east and wrote again for an appointment. This time Rockefeller replied—a friendly letter saying unfortunately he would be in South America. But, he went on, "let me suggest that you mail me your proposal. I can assure you it will have the same consideration it would receive if you brought it to me personally."

I was, frankly, curious to see the office habitat of the Rockefeller clan. I put my prospectus in my briefcase and went east. On (I believe) the 59th floor of the Rockefeller Plaza I left the elevator and went into a simple, dignified reception room—a few chairs, some good-sized potted plants, and a modestly formal and elderly colored man behind a desk.

"May I help you?"

"I'd like to see Mrs. Smith," I said.

"Do you have an appointment?" the courteous grave voice inquired.

"No, I don't."

"Then may I ask why you wanted to see Mrs. Smith."

"I wanted to give her this,"—holding my envelope out.

"Why," he said, an edge of asperity in his voice, "Mrs. Smith wouldn't come out here to get an envelope. Leave it with me and I'll send it in to her."

I hesitated. After all, I wanted to look beyond a reception desk. The receptionist saw my hesitation. His voice suddenly cut in, sharp as a cross-examiner's in court.

"How old are you?"

I was taken off balance. "Forty-three," I said.

"Hmm," said the colored man. He eyed me. "I've been working for the Rockefellers since before you were born," he said. "You can leave the package with me. I'll see that it gets to Mrs. Smith."

I didn't crawl out of the room physically. But I did mentally. Never before or since have I been put down so effectively.

It became a favorite anecdote of mine. I related it to Jim Lee, whose father once handled public relations affairs for the original John D. Rockefeller. Lee laughed, heartily. "I'll see that Tommy Ross tells Laurance about that," he promised. "It's a great story."

Barnett's Barbs

Luke Barnett, who so fooled the seasoned reporters at my first preview, was often employed in various roles by Walter Chrysler. Tex Colbert told me about the first time—a luncheon of the company board, following a regular meeting. Barnett posed as one of his favorite characters, a waiter with a foreign accent. He worked—by prearrangement—behind Chrysler and the then-sales manager of the company, Joe Fields.

Barnett began annoying Fields—subtly at first, as befitted his technique, by such devices as brushing his chair as he walked by, then more obviously, as by removing his dishes after Fields had barely tasted them—returning them, grumpily, when Fields complained. The climax came when Chrysler asked Fields his opinion of a certain Florida dealer.

"A fine man," said Fields. "Industrious, capable—the kind of dealer we would like to have everywhere."

At this point 'waiter' Barnett interrupted, tapping Fields preemptorily on the shoulder.

"I know that man," interjected Barnett angrily. "He cheats. He robs his customers. If you think he's a good dealer, you must be pretty stupid!"

The Chrysler crew of those days was rough and tough. Fields jumped up and swung a fist at Barnett. Barnett ducked away and managed to fall at the same time. On the floor he shouted:

"You hit me—you hit me! I sue you! I sue Chrysler."

Walter Chrysler's roaring laughter brought Fields back to reality—to realization he had been jobbed.

Builder Kaiser

Henry J. Kaiser went to Washington in 1951 to talk to industrial mobilizer Charles E. Wilson—"engine Charley", from General Electric. Korea was the international problem of the day. They were talking about reactivating the Chalmete (Louisiana) aluminum plant. Wilson asked its capacity.

Kaiser answered, pointing out that it would be the largest primary aluminum facility in the world. Then he added: "Would you like to double that figure?"

A Kaiser associate stepped up the ebullient and always optimistic chairman of the Kaiser enterprises. He said: "take it easy, H. J. Remember, Rome wasn't built in a day."

"I wouldn't know about that," replied Kaiser. "I wasn't running that job."

Kaiser was summoned once before a Senatorial committee to testify on the beginnings of his Kaiser-Frazer Corp. One of the Senators asked him why he had at one time sold $300,000 worth of his company's stock.

"Mr. Senator," said Kaiser, "there comes a time in a man's life when he wants $300,000."

Miami Memories

Miami, where I attended many auto previews and many more labor meetings, always brings back fond and occasional wry memories.

Perhaps the most unusual occurred in February of 1972. Walking up the wide central stairway in the Americana Hotel one noon, I half-stumbled on the top step, but caught myself on the balustrade. As I turned at the head of the stairs I saw a rather attractive woman, sitting on the long couch against the rear windows, smiling at my mishap. I walked over to her and said, "I don't usually fall upstairs." I assumed she was the wife of one of the AFL-CIO people at the meeting.

She held up a finger in a "wait" admonition, and pulled a small paper pad from her handbag. She wrote on it and beckoned me to read.

It said, "I am deaf."

I expressed sympathy with a facial gesture. She looked at me and wrote again:

"What are you going to do now?"

I shrugged my shoulders aimlessly.

She wrote: "Would you like to have some fun?"

I was thunderstruck. A deaf and dumb prostitute! I wrote:

"I am tired and all worn out."

She wrote: "Give it a try."

I smiled and nodded 'no'. I decided nobody would ever believe this bizarre episode, so I excused myself with a gesture and went into the Carioca room. There I found Tom Joyce of Newsweek and asked him to peer around the corner to confirm the situation.

I returned and sat down beside the woman. She was pleasantly dressed, nails well manicured, hair well coiffed. She pulled out the pad again and wrote:

"Are you with convention?"

I nodded, and she went on: "How do you like Miami?"

I wrote that I enjoyed Miami always and asked if she did.

She wrote: "I prefer Europe—Germany."

I wrote: "I like Spain."

She wrote: "I have been to Barcelona."

That seemed to end the 'conversation'. We sat in silence a moment. Then I wrote: "I must go now—I'm bad for your business."

She wrote: "I need it."

I left. The next day the Wall Street Journal, having verified the story which immediately flew around the Council meeting, had a paragraph about an anonymous me on the front page. A year later I was still being asked about the incident. I never saw the lady again.

Years earlier some mixup occurred in my reservations and, in the midst of the Miami winter season, I could get a room only at a motel quite distant from the Americana. So I arranged with Joe Gambatese, then of Nation's Business, to use his room as a headquarters for me—I left swim trunks there, so I could hobnob with the labor nabobs on the beach. It was a double-barreled mistake.

The first error was mine. The Gambatese room was on the eighth floor of the Americana Annex, just past a turn in the corridor. I got off the elevator one day, walked past the turn and put the key in the door. Inside I paused—something had changed. My little bag of belongings wasn't against the wall in its accustomed place. I opened the closet to see if Joe or the maid had moved it, and saw an assortment of strange clothes, women's included. I turned back in perplexity—and at that instant a key turned in the door and a man and a woman stood there.

I was petrified—and in a most awkward position. Fortunately, they were as upset as I. I spoke up quickly, "I guess I'm in the wrong room"—and rushed past them. I got onto the elevator and off the floor before they could have called the hotel protection people. I had gotten off one floor before eight—and the room key fitted.

A night later, having partied through most of the night before and needing sleep before a dance contest in which I had foolishly been inveigled, I was napping on Joe's bed when the door opened, the lights came on, there stood Joe and two attractive girls. He was grinning broadly.

I snatched at the slacks I had taken off and sat up. "What's happening?"

One of the girls said, "Are you Mr. Roberts?"

I shook my head no, still a little sleep befogged.

"I guess we're in the wrong place," the girl said. "May I use your phone?"

She did, got another room number, and the two of them left. But before they left she said—"You might want us, so here's my card." She left it on the night table.

"They were at the door when I got here," he said. "They were call girls, and said they were coming to my room—so I figured you must have called them."

I went back to sleep. The next day I decided I must have dreamed the whole episode—until I looked on the night table and there saw the girl's card—name, address, phone number.

Labor editor Asher Lauren of the Detroit News was one of the few Finns in the newsgathering community.

At a labor convention in Miami he sat overlong in a bar making conversation with an attractive young lady. I walked by.

"Come over, Stanley," said Asher. "I want you to meet a friend of mine. This is Louise."

I said how do you do.

"We are talking Finnish," Asher said.

"Ve are not," said Louise in a heavy accent. "Ve are talking Hungarian."

How to Make Good

At the summer meeting of the Society of Automotive Engineers at French Lick in June of 1951, I was playing around the golf course alone one morning when I fell in with R. K. Evans, promoted to a GM executive vice presidency some months earlier, and Harold L. Hamilton, vice president and executive of the Electro-Motive Division. They suggested I join them for the last four or five holes, and I did.

The 18th hole on the valley course at French Lick was slightly uphill, 345 yards long, with a wide fairway. Evans, badly nearsighted, got off a solid straight drive right down the middle of the fairway, about half way to the green. I found myself off at one side in a little trouble, and my second shot did not get me too far. My third shot was to the edge of the green, and meanwhile Evans was rifling his second shot directly to the flag, on a straight line. The ball landed short of the green, and rolled up onto it, about a yard in from the edge.

I walked up to the green with him; he was lying 2 and I was lying 3. I turned to him and said, "That was a beautiful second shot, Mr. Evans."

He looked at me. What he next said he did not say with rancor, nor in a spirit of reprimand, nor unpleasantly and least of all as a joke. But he did say, rather flatly: "It was ten yards short."

I realized that was a good formula for becoming an executive vice president of General Motors.

Persuasion

As president of U.S. Steel, Ben Fairless was the speaker at a Waldorf-Astoria banquet in 1951. He told about a time when, during Charles Schwab's presidency, his company planned a new mill. Purchase began on the large tract of land that was needed. Eventually all the parcels inside the tract were collected except one. The farmer who owned it refused to sell—he turned down more money, company stock, doubled acreage elsewhere; he simply had a sentimental attachment to his land.

Schwab was a most persuasive person. He went to call on the farmer at his home, and they sat down together on the parlor sofa. Charlie put his arm around the farmer's shoulder and turned on the full voltage of his electric personality. He began to talk. He had talked only a short time when the farmer jumped up.

"Mr. Schwab," he said, "I'll sell you the property, but thank God, I'm not a woman."

Getting Results

During World War II, the Cleveland Graphite Bronze Co. was an important supplier of bearings for aircraft programs as well as many others. Like virtually all suppliers of virtually all components, the Cleveland company was generally behind the military's hard delivery schedules.

On this account it was not unusual for the phone to ring in the office of James L. Myers, president, with complaints about deliveries made personally by Lt. Gen. William S. Knudsen, who had taken over procurement during a leave from his presidency at General Motors.

"Mr. Myers," the general would expostulate, "you are behind on your bearings shipments. You're holding up the B-17 program."

Myers would apologize. "We'll get the shipments going faster," he would promise. And then, because plant capacity and materials availability was such that it was impossible to get ahead on the B-17 deliveries without falling even farther behind on other priority shipments, he would make only a perfunctory followup on the problem.

The calls came fairly regularly. "Mr. Myers, we are behind. . . ." And the company president would again apologize and salve the feelings of the procurement chief.

But occasionally the phone would ring and the general's complaint would be voiced thus: "Myers, we're behind on those bearings. We need them right away."

In recounting the story later, Mr. Myers' eyes twinkled. "When he stopped calling me Mr. Myers, and simply called me Myers, I knew he was in real trouble. Whenever that happened we turned the place upside down, and the bearings he wanted moved ahead of everything else."

Plumbing the Depths

Reporter Tom Nicholson, as well as being a quick thinker, was a capable mimic. Out at the Auto Union's Solidarity House one day he heard that Red Roche of the union's legal department was being considered for the post of Director of Saline Water in John Kennedy's administration. He had Isabelle Valdez of the public relations department, whom he later married, call Roche's office, get him on the line and tell him the White House was calling.

Nicholson then took the phone. In a fair imitation of President Kennedy's voice, he sweetly inquired: "Is this my new director of saline water?"

Roche answered, trembling. "Yes, Mr. President."

Nicholson became more brusque. "Fine," he said. "Get over to the White House right away. We're having trouble with one of the upstairs toilets."

Flint Frolicking

One of the larger poker games used to take place among Flint General Motors executives at the top of the Durant Hotel, in the Flint City Club. As an official and later general manager of Buick, Ed Ragsdale periodically waged a war of nerves in the high stakes game. He would pull out a thousand dollar bill (he customarily carried three or four of them) and ask if anyone had change.

Another player in the game was walking by his bank and saw on display a $10,000 bill. Seized with an idea, he went in to the president's office, arranged to borrow it, signed a note for it and went away, ready to outgame Ragsdale.

As it happened, Ragsdale, too, came into the bank a short time later. The president, not knowing the situation, related to Ragsdale how their friend had borrowed the $10,000 bill. Ragsdale realized what was impending.

"How many thousand dollar bills do you have?" he asked. He went into his wallet and found he had three. "I need seven."

They were procured from the vault, and Ragsdale went on his way. The game started. After a time the friend opened his wallet and pulled out the $10,000 note.

"Anybody got change?" he inquired casually.

"Well, let's see," said Ragsdale. He dug into his pocket, counted out his ten $1,000 bills and picked up the big one.

Ragsdale was himself an occasional victim, as in an incident some years earlier, when he was assistant chief engineer. He was driving a test car to Detroit when he was overhauled by a state policeman. The officer looked at Ragsdale's driver's license, then asked for the car registration.

"This is a Buick test car," said Ragsdale. "I don't have a registration for it."

"Well," said the officer, "we'd better go into town and check that."

"No need of that," replied Ragsdale. "Some other Buick people are coming down, too. They'll be here in a few minutes—they'll vouch for this."

Another company car approached and the officer flagged it down. Driving was O.W. Young, Buick's factory manager—who ranked Ragsdale those days.

The officer related Ragsdale's story to him. Young looked at Ragsdale, then back at the officer.

"Never saw him before in my life," he declared—and drove on.

The Long Trips

Three vivid reporting experiences have become part of my remembrances, the result of long trips and deep insights.

The first of these was when Army Ordnance invited me, as Detroit bureau chief for McGraw-Hill, to travel to Korea in early 1952 to see materiel from conception to use. The trip began at Detroit, thence to Aberdeen Proving Grounds, Lima Ordnance Depot, Texarkana Depot, San Francisco, Anchorage and cold weather back-country testing, Tokyo, Masan, Seoul, the battlefront, Midway, Hawaii and home.

At the front we drove in convoy down a valley, ranges on both sides. The driver, a private, leaned back. "I don't like this a damned bit," he said.

"Why?"

He pointed to the right. "The gooks are up on that ridge."

We arrived at a hill on the left and cut back behind it. A captain came down and glared at our colonel in charge. "They were shelling that road a half-hour ago," he said.

We walked up the hill to the artillery spotting observation post. I drifted back down to hear our colonel talking to the jeep drivers: "You will proceed back 200 yards apart. If anyone is hit, you will not stop—someone else will get them. Travel as fast as you can."

I wondered why I was there—bad enough to be there under orders, but to simply visit! We got back all right. I wondered for a long time thereafter what happened that night when the gooks sent out scouts to find out why our procession had come and gone at that observation post. Poor victims of our curiosity!

Years later, after I bought Air and Water News from McGraw-Hill in late 1970, the United Nations summoned an Environmental Conference in Stockholm for a two-week period in June of 1972. As publisher of an environmental letter, I attended. Great people of all the world's nations—121 of them, at least—were there. Ministers of state came and went. I photographed Indira Gandhi, a smiling, competent, pleasant woman, at close range. (Afterward, at a press conference, she took questions in Indian, German and English, translated where necessary into English, and replied in the language of the inquiry—smoothly, carefully, pleasantly.) Another time King Gustav Adolf V of Sweden left his limousine and walked into the Opera House; I stood a few feet from him in a group questioning him; he was relaxed and easy—unguarded.

The conference lasted a time-filled two weeks. In between the continual meetings we correspondents (more than 1,000) were royally entertained. A monumental buffet dinner in the City Hall square, with tables of regional specialties. A boat trip to Sandhamn Yacht Club, scene of international sailing races, on the edge of the Swedish-Finnish border. I flew to Goteburg to see Volvo car research work. Superb restaurants. Everything most expensive.

I broke the work with a one-day visit to Helsinki—walking, sightseeing, shopping, eating.

No less exciting, though milder, was my excursion into the South Pacific in 1965, following the footsteps of an Auto Union contingent Walter Reuther had sent to Australia to help the Vehicle Workers Union there handle some bargaining problems—and to probe to see if Reuther could possibly assume leadership of a worldwide automotive labor structure.

The AFL-CIO convention in San Francisco was finishing the day I took off via Qantas for Hawaii, the Fijis and Sydney. There General Motors took me in hand with a car and driver; I talked with union and company people for three days, then went on to Melbourne for more conversations. (There, at the U.S. legation, the labor attache's secretary asked me over the phone who I was; when I identified myself as Labor Trends, she warmed my heart with, "Oh, we know Labor Trends. We get it in the diplomatic pouch each week." Which every labor attache did, around the world.)

From Melbourne back to Sydney, thence to Wellington, where Ford people shepherded me. I spent Christmas at Weirakei, halfway up to Auckland—steamy geysers around us; Maoris; friendly but reserved New Zealanders as well. From Auckland to Tahiti for a few days, thence Mexico City and New Year's Eve before flying back to Detroit.

Mottisms

Charles S. Mott, for a long time the largest individual stockholder in General Motors, had the entrepreneur's pejorative attitude for the manager—the man who did the work. I ran into him one day while I was doing a profile on Harlow H. Curtice, the new president of General Motors. I asked Mott why Curtice had been chosen president ahead of other officers.

"For one thing," said Mott, "whenever a vacancy opened up above Harlow, he was such an outstanding choice that there was nothing to do but select him. And besides that, he's a damned fool."

I was startled. "I'm afraid I don't follow you, Mr. Mott," I said.

"Well," said Mr. Mott, "look at it this way. Two years back I invested in a water company. I put about four million dollars in it. It's a great company—doesn't pay any dividends, plows the money back into the business. Today that four million dollar investment is worth six million."

He paused and looked at me. "Look!" he said, almost scornfully. "Imagine how long it takes Curtice to earn two million dollars!"

Mr. Mott was widely known as a penurious man. For the wedding reception of one of his daughters, he (quite possibly reluctantly) ordered the least expensive champagne available, with the stipulation that he could return whatever was not consumed of the many cases. After the wedding he appeared at the store for refund of the surplus—one bottle!

We got acquainted in the early fifties when I did a profile of him for Business Week. One day soon after, as I was walking through the AC Spark Plug plant in Flint on a press tour, he came in a side door, saw my familiar face and fell in step with me at the end of the procession. We talked of this and that, notably some of his investments, and he told me about a recent purchase of an interest in a water company.

That was when I was thinking about starting a magazine dealing with the auto industry. I said, "Mr. Mott, maybe I should come up and talk with you about an idea I have that requires some financing. It's a good idea, and I need about a quarter of a million dollars."

Mott looked sidewise at me with a gleam of genuine alarm on his face. Then he jumped—physically jumped—a yard sideways. We kept walking along a yard apart in what turned out to be a considerable silence for a time. Then gradually he narrowed the distance between us, and our conversation resumed. But I never went back to my financing suggestion.

No Smoking

For most of the years of his working life, Fred Zeder was a convivial soul—a heavy smoker and social drinker. In his later years his doctor ordered him off cigarettes and liquor, and Zeder decided what was good for him was good for everybody else. He ordered 1,000 "no smoking" signs and hung them all around Chrysler's engineering building in Highland Park. He saw to it that the rules were enforced.

There was one exception to his rule. K.T. Keller, then president of the company, would periodically stride into the engineering department. He would go into one vest pocket for a cigarette and put it in his mouth, presumably with his eye on whatever was the object of his attention. He would put the other hand in his other vest pocket and bring out a kitchen match of the kind he customarily carried. Then, with his eye apparently still concentrated on his objective but still, nevertheless, with Zeder in his view, he would sidle over to the nearest "no smoking" sign, strike the match on it with a great flourish, and light his cigarette.

What It Takes

As president of Chrysler, K.T. Keller was always most highly regarded as a production man. Of the many compliments paid him on that score, however, none was ever more flattering than that which came from Andrew J. Langhammer, chief of the Chrysler Oilite powdered metals division—a more profound compliment because it was intended simply as an observation.

Langhammer told me how he and Keller went to Washington at the start of World War II to look over various products Ordnance wanted manufactured. Ordnance had put these parts up on boards; they extended along a wall about 100 feet long.

"Keller and I slowly walked down past all those pieces," Langhammer related. "We would stop, and Keller would say, 'We can make this one at Oilite.' Then we'd walk a little beyond and Keller would say, 'We can make this one, too.' It took us about 15 minutes to go down the length of the board, and during that time Keller picked five pieces which my division could manufacture. He turned to me and said, 'There's your assignment.'"

Langhammer paused, then went on. "I spent the next three days studying that couple hundred pieces on those boards. It turned out that Oilite could make the five pieces Keller had picked out—and I'll be Goddamned because after three days of studying I couldn't find another single piece we could do!"

Presidents

As a child of eight I saw Woodrow Wilson in a parade up Fifth Avenue as he returned from Versailles and the peacemaking of the first World War; I was perched excitedly on the hard roof of the family Cole, providentially halted right at Fifth Avenue as we were driving across town. Once I saw Franklin D. Roosevelt, twice John Kennedy. But I never spoke to a president till Lyndon Johnson occupied the White House.

My then-new wife and I were in Washington. We ran into Ethel and Leon Loeb and joined them for lunch in the Democratic Club in the Carlton Hotel. "Have you seen everything you wanted to see?" Ethel asked.

"Everything except the White House," my bride replied.

"Oh, my," said Ethel. Then typically: "Would you want to see it this afternoon? We're going to a reception there."

We nodded surprised assent. Ethel bustled off to call someone. She returned. "It's all set," she said. "Meet us at the East Gate at five o'clock."

We waited there, and a bus drew up. Ethel waved from a window. "Come on," she said. We found a seat behind her on the other side of the aisle. The bus went in to a check point and a guard came aboard. "May I see your invitations, please," he asked.

Alarmed, I nudged Ethel. "Tell him you're the press," she whispered hoarsely.

I was thunderstruck. The guard moved to us. "Your invitation?" he asked.

"I'm a reporter—press," I said.

"May I see your press card?"

I hadn't carried a press card for a score of years. I pretended to look for one, and came up with my Detroit Press Club membership card. I held it out. He looked at it briefly—and went on. "Some security!" I thought.

The President joined the reception some 30 minutes after we arrived. He surveyed the scene and—having an eye for attractive blondes—made a beeline across the room to my wife. He engaged her in animated conversation for five minutes or so while I stood alongside. She recalled to him that they had met when he had come to Detroit some months earlier and she had somehow inadvertently found herself in the official receiving line. ("I'm Mrs. Cummings from Missouri," she had told Michigan attorney-general Frank Kelley, to whom she had spoken simply because he wore a "Committee" ribbon. He apparently thought she was important enough to join the receiving line, and escorted her to it.)

The President professed to remember her—maybe he did. Then he drifted on. Liz Carpenter came quickly over.

"Where are you folks from?" she asked.

"Detroit."

"Why," she said, "we get out to Detroit often. We'll call you—you came with the Loebs?—we'll get your number from them." She, too, left.

We mingled—with Ladybird Johnson (with whom my wife had had conversation months before alongside the President's plane), with Sargent Shriver, with a scattering of Senators and Congressmen, and common folk, too. I drank martinis out of Texas-size glasses—actually brandy snifters—and somewhat unsteadily bumped into a table in the Green Room and almost knocked it over. (Minutes later a more unsteady woman did just that.)

We left an hour or so later. Liz Carpenter never did phone.

Securing Situations

When M. E. Coyle resigned as executive vice president of General Motors Corp. late in 1950 many friends came to him and asked him why he had done so, a few years ahead of normal retirement time. He said the horizon was clouding up, that friends of his were dropping dead every day of heart attacks, and that he did not feel up to getting himself pinched into a new job for a possible new war period. He added:

"Another thing, too. When Tom Keating came into my job at Chevrolet, he used to come around to me and ask me what to do. Then he began to come to me and ask if I liked the idea of what he was planning to do. Now he comes to me and tells me what he has done. I don't have to worry about Chevrolet any longer."

The rumor was six months old when it was confirmed—Ben Bidwell became manager of the Ford division in March of 1973. At his first press conference he stood before an audience which included several major Ford officials, including president Lee A. Iacocca, and he had this to say:

"I especially want to pay tribute to three men in this room who were instrumental in effecting my promotion to this new post. I refer to Maynard Gordon of Motor News Analysis, Bob Finlay of Automotive News and Al Fleming of Autoproducts. They insisted for months that I would get the job. Ford listens well, it seems, and their declarations finally proved true!"

Presidential Order

As president of General Motors from 1953 to 1958, Harlow H. Curtice looked every inch a corporate executive—a true movie version. And he was an imperious man, too, a command post operator if ever there was one.

The high point of this side of his character came at Chicago in 1955 when GM sponsored the Powerama—a display of huge earthmoving equipment and other such on the shore of Lake Michigan, spread outdoors for all to see.

A press luncheon and conference came a day before the Powerama was to open—a gray day, with a broad hint of rain in the air. Halfway through the session came a question born of the clammy feel of the weather:

"Mr. Curtice, suppose it rains tomorrow? What then?"

Curtice drew himself up as though offended at the question. He stared at the questioner and replied coldly:

"It will not rain!"

It didn't.

Bonus

Christian Girl was the truly improbable name of a man who bulked large in the early days of the auto industry—his initials were used to name the CG Spring Bumper Co., which he created and which later became the basis of Houdaille-Hershey. We met when he was in his late seventies, sometime before the start of World War II. He was at that time trying to get into high gear a little company whose product I do not recall.

We talked about the early days of the auto industry. He said:

"I was responsible for Billy Durant regaining control of General Motors back in 1919."

I asked for details. He went on:

"Durant was only a little bit short of getting control back after he lost it to the du Ponts. There was a block of a few thousand shares in Toledo which belonged to a friend of mine. Durant called me in and told me to go down to Toledo and get a proxy for those shares.

"They were strategic shares, because they belonged to an influential man in Toledo and a number of other people would go the way he went. I came back with his proxy for Durant, and others then flowed in from there. Durant regained control."

He paused. "Know what he did for me?"

I shook my head.

"He gave me 75,000 shares of Chevrolet."

I don't know what Chevrolet stock was worth in those days. But obviously it was well worth a day's travel to Toledo.

Victories

Sometimes there were triumphs. Ray Sackett of the Society of Automotive Engineers whispered to me during the tire-short days of World War II that he had heard du Pont and Thiokol had perfected a new approach to synthetic rubber tires and would build a plant on the outskirts of Wilmington to produce their development. I had just started freelancing for Business Week. I reported my news to New York. Presumably the editors wanted to look me over—they suggested I uncover the story myself in the east.

I began in Detroit with U. S. Rubber. Careful probings established to my satisfaction they knew nothing of the development. I went to Trenton, New Jersey, where the Thiokol plant was located—no luck; my target there professed himself unable to see me. I went to Washington and probed again at the governmental office in charge—carefully, for I was afraid to reveal what I knew, for fear the story would seep all across Washington. Nothing was said to confirm my tip.

Discouraged, I took the train to Wilmington and sat down in the office of one Henry Ford, chief of Du Pont development. I asked a number of question about synthetic rubber developments—what du Pont was doing—and so on. Ford professed to know nothing of any important new turns.

Rebuffed, I sat silent a moment. Then I said, "If you have no new developments, then why are you and Thiokol planning to build a plant to make your new synthetic?"

Ford's face showed how stunned he was. Long silence. Then he said, "Well, I guess you know." Then he gave me the story. Business Week had an exclusive beat on what at that time was major news—and it cemented me into a new job.

Another Ford—Henry II—and I became well acquainted very shortly after he moved into the affairs of the family company. He impressed me early with his grasp of matters which should have been strange to him—the identification of machines, for example, whose pictures he showed me being installed at Poissy, in the Ford of France operations. Our relationship warmed and ripened.

There came a day when he told me the company was going to end its long relationship with Ferguson Tractor. "We've lost a lot of money on that deal," he said. "When the contract terminates in a few months it won't be renewed." We talked about some details of the situation.

I was the Detroit editor for Business Week. I returned to my office and wrote what was at the time a decidedly important story for that publication. It created waves.

One wave crested in my office. My telephone rang the Monday morning the story appeared. Roger Kyes, the tractor operation president, another man with whom I had long had fine relationships, spoke to me in tones of Wagnerian tragedy.

"Stanley, did you write that story in Business Week today?"

"Yes, Roger, I did."

"You never came to me to talk about it."

"Roger, I didn't think there was anything you could add."

"You should have talked with me."

"Is the story wrong?—are any of the facts wrong?"

"That's not the point." The voice became sharp, bitter. "I am just amazed that after the respect we have had for each other—the confidence we have had in each other—that you would print a story like that before talking with me!"

And more. We finished, and I decided that marked the end of a friendship. But at Christmas time I got a card from Kyes from somewhere in the south Pacific, and I decided maybe the rupture wasn't as bad as I had believed.

Some five years later a man came up to me at a reception and said, "Remember me?"

I knew the face but couldn't identify him.

"I was the publicity director for Ferguson Tractor."

"Now I remember," I said.

"Do you recall the day you had that Business Week story about Ford breaking off with Ferguson?"

I acknowledged I remembered it well.

He said: "I began leafing through Business Week that morning and the story hit me in the face. I rushed in to Kyes. I asked him if he knew anything about the story. He said he did. Then he said, 'Get Stanley on the phone. I want to talk to him.'"

"I asked him if there were errors we could move in on. He shook his head no. I asked him why he was going to call you. He just said, 'I'm going to chew him out.'"

At Ferguson Kyes had a story he liked to tell—how one tractor could do the work of a certain number of horses, and thus save feed for those horses that would require cultivating a large amount of acreage. The figures were thoroughly familiar to me.

A McGraw-Hill editors' meeting took place at Detroit, with General Motors people as guests. The GM president of that day, in the course of a discourse on mechanization, began talking of the virtues of tractors—and he used the figures I knew so well on horses, grain and acreage.

I confronted him afterward. "Has General Motors been talking with Roger Kyes about an executive position?" I asked.

The GM officer fumbled with his reply. He admitted, obliquely, to conversations. I had what I needed.

Sometimes the reporter falls into luck. I had a date for breakfast in Chicago with Paul Hoffman while he was president of Studebaker as World War II was ending. It so happened that a major auto industry meeting had been scheduled for Washington the day before, and I feared Hoffman would break the date. But he didn't, and we sat down at the Illinois Athletic Club.

I had to write a story, of course, on the closed-door auto meeting. That morning, I bought all the available papers, but their versions of what had gone on were completely at variance with one another. I asked Hoffman what had happened. He told me he had sent Courtney Johnson to represent him and hadn't heard from him yet.

I showed him the clippings of the stories—all different. He smiled.

"Judging from what's been written here, I'd guess they were covering up and what they decided was this—and this—and this." He went down the list of probabilities.

We finished breakfast. I returned to my hotel and called the head of the Automobile Manufacturers Association in Detroit, George Romney.

"What happened yesterday in Washington, George?"

"Stan, I don't know. I wasn't allowed in the meeting. I sat outside with the reporters."

"Well," I said, "it seems to me they would have had to discuss such-and-such—and that the decisions would have been thus-and-thus."

Silence at the other end. Then a hesitant reply. "Now that you mention it, there was some talk on the train last night to that effect. I guess that's right."

"And, George, wouldn't they have talked about this—and this? And the answer to that one would have been so-and-so?"

Reluctant confirmation again. I went down my list of Hoffman probabilities, and Romney had to confirm them all. I hung up exultant.

At the other end in Romney's office was a man I knew. He told me afterward: "Romney hung up and said to me, 'that was Brams and he was over in Chicago and he knew everything that went on in Washington. Where in hell did he learn all that?' "

Sidetracks

The first explosive word of the recession of 1938 came in a General Motors press conference announcing the indefinite layoff of 100,000 men. Harlan Hadley, then Wall Street Journal chief in Detroit, and I had something else that we wanted to learn. We rode up to the GM building in a cab framing a series of questions that would drive president William S. Knudsen into a corner where he'd have to answer.

The press conference began; the layoff announcement was made; and bedlam occurred for a time—after which the conference resumed. Soon Hadley dropped in the first question of our sequence. Knudsen answered. I asked about some implications; Knudsen was being driven to a corner. GM's press chief, Felix Bruner, saw where the questions were going. He puffed furiously on his cigar, but he could say nothing as Hadley bored in with the next question.

Knudsen was on the ropes, ready for the kill. I opened my mouth. But at that instant, The Detroit Times' Vera Brown, an embodiment of the storybook 'sob sister' of a near-legendary school, broke in. She was obviously bored with complicated, stuffy business questions.

"Mr. President," she cried, her hand upraised. "Have you a message for the young men of today?"

We were derailed. We never got back. I will always remember Felix Bruner, across from me, exhaling an enormous mouthful of smoke, convulsively, happily.

Every reporter can give you parallel examples. I remember Bert Pierce, the New York Herald-Tribune auto editor, at a press conference at the Chrysler proving grounds in 1953. Someone had made a slip and remarked on a sale of trucks to China—a story of international importance in those days of boycotting of China. Pierce interrupted the digging into that revelation with a question of another sort: "What's this I hear about deer on the proving ground roads?"

Best Wishes

At the first press showing of the then-new Oldsmobile Toronado model, in July of 1965, Ralph Watts of the Detroit News was making an heroic effort to learn in which price bracket the car would be sold. He asked direct and indirect questions but got nowhere. Finally he said to H. N. Metzel, the general manager of the division: "I just want to get some idea on the price."

Metzel looked at him and smiled pleasantly. "I hope you're successful," he said.

A Prophet's Lot in His Own Country

Before Al Nute became a publicist for Graham-Paige and later Dodge truck he had served a long apprenticeship as an editor of the Toledo Times—and as a reporter before that.

In 1928 Lita Gray Chaplin was quoted as saying that as part of her divorce action against Charlie Chaplin she would testify he was a moron. Chaplin was traveling east at that time. Reporter Al boarded the train at Toledo, learned Chaplin's whereabouts and rapped on the door. Chaplin asked who it was. Nute identified himself as a reporter, and Chaplin said he did not want to talk to the press.

"Just a moment, Mr. Chaplin," said Nute through the door. "Let me read you the Associated Press story that just came to my office." He read the offensive section.

Chaplin opened the door. "This is terrible," he said. "Come in."

He made explanations to Nute, and the conversation expanded. The conductor rapped on the door and asked Nute for his fare from Toledo to Cleveland. Nute found he had far too few dollars with him.

"How much do you need?" Chaplin inquired.

"I guess about ten dollars," Nute replied. Chaplin handed him a bill. Nute paid the conductor and wrote Chaplin a check for the amount—a check the comedian never cashed.

At Cleveland Nute went immediately to the Plain Dealer office, borrowed a typewriter and hurried into the interview he had had—the only interview Chaplin ever gave on his situation. The A.P. broke the story into a six-part release, and moved it on its national wire. It drew widespread acceptance, coast to coast.

Back in Toledo the then editor of the Toledo Times was, like Chaplin, in the midst of a divorce action. Sensitive, he had given orders that no divorce stories of any sort were to run in the Times. Nute's scoop made front pages nationwide—but it never appeared in his own newspaper.

Layout Formula

One of the officials of Jarecki Machine & Tool Co., Grand Rapids, once worked for William S. Knudsen when Knudsen was the production head of General Motors. This man was laying out a new plant, and asked Knudsen for advice on how to place the machines. Knudsen said, "It's simple. Just point all their noses toward the delivery door." Anyone who examines a well conceived production plant will see that this homely metaphor has been followed out.

Stupe

He shall be nameless here, because doltishness to that degree deserves no publicizing, but I will note that he was a divisional industrial relations manager. My wife and I met him and his wife in New York during an auto show of the late forties. Because he had done me a favor and was a Labor Trends reader in the early days of that publication, we took them in tow.

By a chain of involved circumstances, I had entree and recognition those days at "21." As we talked of a possible place for an after-theatre drink, I said, "I know where we'll go." I gave the address to the cab driver, and we were welcomed and taken to a good table.

There we each had a drink, a juicy, fat hamburger and coffee. The tab was a bit more than thirty dollars, and the tip was on top of that—large outlay indeed for me in those days, but I was gratified by the way I had shown my guest I was surely an important man, accustomed to the upper reaches of entertainment. I was still brimming in my self-satisfaction when we dropped them off at their hotel and went on to ours.

The euphoria wore off, but the inner contentment continued. For a month, that is. At that point I met my guest in downtown Detroit. He clapped me on the shoulder.

"I'm so glad to see you," he said. "What was the name of that hamburger joint we went to in New York?"

My stomach still turns over when I recall the incident.

The Beefeaters

In April of 1960 I flew from Miami to Jamaica with my family. Returning a week later, I bought duty-free Beefeater gin and brought it back to Bloomfield Hills. When I opened our first bottle it seemed milder than the variety I usually had—and there was no proof rating on the label. Out of curiosity I wrote the importer to inquire if the Jamaican variety had the same strength as that in Michigan liquor stores.

Rudy Kopf of Kobrand wrote back. Yes, he said, it was the same. And he went on: If you fancy Beefeater gin, you may well want to join the Beefeater Club. He enclosed a membership application which I filled out and returned. Thus, as I later have widely proclaimed, I became a big man in gin!

First a yeoman, then, for some reason I knew not, the bailiff of the Central Bailiwick. A gold medal went with the bailiffship. The first Beefeater banquet was held at White's in lower New York, on Oct. 30, 1963. I was there. In 1968 I became the Upper Warder of the Central Bailiwick, leader of some 150 Beefeaters in the Great Lakes area.

I held that post for six years, during which I made many acquaintances countrywide, many warm friendships. With my fellow Upper Warders—Phil Milner of the East, John Knox of the West, Keith Kelly of the South—I participated in a score of ceremonies at dinners—the passing of the Keys, the questioning of the initiates, the traditions of fellowship and great food at the banquets. My good friend, Chief Warder Rudy Kopf, later Governor, led these ceremonies, enlivened by the wit of Reeve (later Chief Warder) Whitney Gerard.

I had the great pleasure of seeing son John initiated into the fellowship at the Bath Club in Miami on Feb. 26, 1973, along with Hugo L. Black, Jr. I had the tingling thrill of dining at the first Tower of London Beefeater dinner in 1970, there seeing and hearing the original 700-year-old ceremony of the Passing of the Keys at the Tower entrance—chill night, peremptory challenge and recognition of the oncoming Guard (crisp, ringing words in the nocturnal silence), locking of the ponderous gate. Then a repeat at the Tower in 1975, me then an Upper Warder Emeritus.

Food fit for the gods at a long procession of banquets—from Miami to Boston to San Francisco, to many points in between. Always the Question could be answered in the affirmative: "Have the traditions of good food and fellowship been upheld here tonight at this Beefeater dinner?"

Working

The Society of Older Graduates, a Columbia group of which I have the honor to be a member, always attracts a blue ribbon audience to its black tie annual dinners. In 1975 the president of the University, Dr. William J. McGill, remarked that he had lately spent a week in Iran studying educational facilities as the guest of the oil-rich government. "The problems of university administration these days often center around money and contributions," he said. "I was walking down the street in Teheran and someone called hello. It turned out to be John R. Hubbard, the president of the University of Southern California. He asked, 'how long have you been working this territory?'"

Dining Out

In 1958 I dined one night at the Bloomfield Hills Country Club with Edge Austin, who then ran the Detroit office of Timken Roller Bearing Co. I was telling Edge how I had spent most of the previous night playing poker and had won three dollars. "Imagine," I said, "up all night and only three dollars for my time!"

"That's better than losing the three dollars," said a voice. We turned and it proved to be John Gordon, then a group executive of General Motors.

Gordon was eating by himself, and quietly. When we finished we turned to his table, stood there a moment talking, then went on our way.

Three days later he was announced as the new president of General Motors—something he naturally knew at the time we met. It occurred to me at the time of the announcement that the solitary dinner of three evenings before probably marked the last time he would be able to eat uninterrupted by an endless throng who wanted to shake his hand.

The difficulties of eating alone when you are a celebrity were epitomized by Jimmy Hoffa. While he was president of the Teamsters Union I was working on a profile of him for The Saturday Evening Post, and we lunched from time to time at Carl's Chop House. I would meet him at the door, but it would be a full 30 minutes before we were able to get to a table, so numerous were the interruptions by other diners who had something they wanted to say to Hoffa. Luncheon, too, was slow—the interruptions were nearly endless.

Age's Attributes

Boss Kettering had a sly sense of humor, and it never evidenced itself more notably than at one of a series of Fisher Body Craftsmen's Guild dinners in the early 1960s.

Each year Fisher awarded prizes and scholarships to the best designers of, first, replicas of the Fisher royal coach trademark, and later, model cars. The awards were made at large dinners attended by topmost General Motors officials.

Kettering was introduced at one of these for a few remarks directed to the young prize winners.

"I have just one word of advice for you young people," he said in his high-pitched voice. "Whenever you have a problem, consult with your elders. People older than you have had more experience, and they are able to give you the benefit of that experience."

In his late seventies, the Boss looked down the table and fastened his eye on fellow GM director Charles S. Mott, a few months older than he.

"I follow that same practice myself," he told the crowded banquet room. "When I need advice I go and seek it from my elder, Stewart Mott!"

Mott straightened up, pique at this jibe crossing his face. A subdued chuckle went around the room as Kettering, seemingly impervious to his 'elder's' reaction, placidly continued speaking.

At the celebration of his 75th birthday in Dayton, Kettering related some of the events leading up to the development of the high compression engine which came out of the General Motors Research Laboratories about three years earlier. When he first assigned the project, he said, the technicians to whom he gave it were so dubious of the principles involved that they had no stomach whatsoever for the job. They even asked him for a letter instructing them to work on it. Kettering told them:

"I will write such a letter, but I won't sign it. If the job is going to be as bad as you say, if the theories are as wrong as you say, then working on it won't soil your lily-white reputations. And if it's as good as I know it is, you won't want any such letter."

The research went on, and the development brought out the initial high compression engine. It went down south for running road tests. When the 50,000-mile test was reported up to General Motors Central Offices, a postscript was appended on Kettering's copy. It said: "There's nothing new in this as far as you're concerned, but it's a hell of a shock to the rest of us."

Change-Room Babies

In 1942 Glenn Cummings and I crossed northern Ontario in search of stories, he for The Wall Street Journal, I for the Chicago Journal of Commerce. At Timmins, Ont., we were taken with pride by the McIntyre-Porcupine people through their change room facilities. It was explained to us how the men came up from the mine at the end of the day, got undressed, went through a shower corridor where the water changed progressively from hot to cold, thence to a moving belt bordered with ultra-violet lamps, so while they dried off they could get some of the sunlight they missed during the day. The belt wound around to where they put on their street clothes and went home.

This facility, characteristic of the paternalistic attitude of the big gold mine, went into operation in 1935. Within a year the birth rate of Timmins jumped explosively. Miners were no longer returning home weary, dirty and jaded. The population explosion continued abnormally high for about two years, then tapered back toward normal.

Any miner's child born in that first birth burst became known as a change room baby. Even the school teachers used the expression: "He's a change room boy." "She's a change room child."

I sent Reader's Digest the anecdote. But this was in the early forties. It came back with the word that even though it was highly appreciated, it probably was not the kind of material the Digest could print.

Baseball

John W. Davis told about the first World Series broadcasting contract, signed while he was sales vice president of Ford.

"I began to think about the possibility of sponsoring World Series broadcasts, and made arrangements to see Judge Landis. I went to him in Chicago after an appointment was made, and told him my story. He sat very quietly and did not say a word, and at the end said: 'I will have to think about this for a few days.'

"I telephoned him in a few days and he asked me to come over. I went over and sat down. He said: 'In order to sponsor the World Series on a broadcast, you will have to do two things. You will have to pay us $100,000 beyond the cost of the network time you use, and you will have to submit to me all the commercials you plan to use. I do not want you to be putting beans in the ears of all our listeners.'

"I said: 'We plan to use only about three minutes of commercials during the whole program.'

"He said: 'How can I be sure of that?'

"I said: 'We can write it into the contract.'

"He said: 'Well, that won't be necessary. If you say so, that is good enough.'

"So we signed the agreement and paid the $100,000. We did this for three years. Shortly after I signed the contract for the fourth year Frank Campsall, then secretary to Mr. Henry Ford, telephoned me. He said: 'Mr. Ford doesn't want to sponsor the World Series this year.'

"I told him that it was already too late—that I had signed a contract.

"He said: 'Can't you get out of it?'

"I replied: 'I guess I can, but it will cost us some money.'

"I called Judge Landis. I went to see him and told him the story. He said: 'So Mr. Ford doesn't want to sponsor the Series this year?'

"I said: 'That's right.'

"He said: 'Does he understand that will cost him $100,000?'

"I said: 'Yes, he does. But isn't there some way we can get out of this—will it be all right if we find a substitute?'

"He agreed that would be permissible if the substitute was acceptable to him.

"I got in touch with the agency people—N. W. Ayer & Sons. But they had only six days in which to operate, and they couldn't find a substitute. The World Series was not sponsored that year, although we had paid the $100,000 for rights. The next year Gillette took over the sponsorship."

Epitaph

Charles Sorensen was hard-boiled like nobody before or since when he ran the Rouge works of the Ford Motor Co. Finished there when the elder Ford's regime came to its end, he later joined Willys-Overland—and then visibly relaxed and softened.

When he died, Bill Sherman of the Automobile Manufacturers Association recalled a curious remark Sorensen made after leaving Ford:

"The bricks and mortar were so much they made you sick every morning."

Pistol Packing Papa

Howard Handleman was Detroit bureau chief of International News Service in the late thirties and early forties. We lived in the same apartment. He told me one night about an interview that morning with Ford's Harry Bennett, the man through whose fingers practically everything passed that happened at the Ford Motor Company.

Handleman had a sensitive subject to probe. He said he talked casually about minor matters for a few moments, then gradually began to edge into the topic he wanted to explore.

Bennett, as always, sat on the small of his back in his chair, his feet sprawled across an outstretched desk drawer. As Handleman got into the basics of his questioning Bennett reached into the open drawer and pulled out a small revolver—the revolver whose existence has been reported in other accounts and questioned in still others. He aimed it at a target somewhere out of sight behind Handleman on the wall of his basement office and pulled the trigger.

Said Howard: "I heard that bullet go by my ear, and I sort of forgot what I was asking about. It took me a few minutes to get back on the track. And when I did, Bennett took aim again, and this time the bullet seemed closer."

Bennett had gone on talking, seemingly encouraging the conversation—actually, of course, closing it off. Howard wasn't hearing what was being said. "Stan, I decided I owed a lot to Mr. Hearst, but there were limits to what I owed. I got up and got out of there."

I edited Ward's Automotive Reports in that period. Getting accurate auto output figures then was a hard job. Al Ward would get Hudson's and Chrysler's, for example, by standing at the plant windows and counting cars going by on the assembly lines over a 30-minute period. He would then check the nearby saloons to find if line speeds had changed at all during the week. Simple multiplication produced the week's total output.

Ford figures were my assignment, gathered from an inside contact. One day I dropped in on Harry Bennett. I pointed out to him that we always got the figures, but that it was sometimes difficult and sometimes wrong—which did not benefit Ford. I asked him if he would provide us with official totals.

He called in his aide, Stan Fay. "Brams will call you every Thursday for the production figures," he said. "Give them to him."

Life on that sector thenceforth became easier. A year later I was in the Ford sales department, talking to an official who suddenly asked:

'Say, where does Ward's get our production figures, anyway?"

I replied that we never told how we got the figures for any company. I asked why he was interested.

"Oh," he said, "Bennett thinks the leak on the figures is in this department. He's been raising hell about it around here."

I admitted that Bennett's actions were interesting indeed.

A Hair-Raising Reply

Harry Bennett's powers were extraordinary, but one day—goes a story, probably apocryphal—he could not locate an executive. That worthy finally turned up a few hours later in Bennett's office. Asked Bennett, obviously irritated:

"Where have you been?"

"Getting a haircut."

"Don't get your hair cut on company time," said Bennett curtly.

The apocryphal part of the story is that the man then replied: "It grew on company time."

"Not all of it," was the supposed retort.

"I didn't have all of it cut off."

Personal Phone Calls

When W. S. Knudsen was president of General Motors in the thirties, he quite often dialed his own numbers.

Volney Fowler, in charge of the then-small Detroit public relations office, picked up his phone one day when it rang, and said the customary hello. The voice on the other end said, in a thick Danish accent, "Dis is Knudsen."

Fowler suspected a joke. "Yeah," he replied, "and dis is Admiral Peary."

The voice came back, a bit pained, "Yeah, but dis IS Knudsen!" And it was.

Many years later a man was again in a commanding place at GM who did his own dialing from time to time. Chairman Richard Gerstenberg one day wanted some material dealing with a lawsuit. He dialed the legal department man who had handled the matter, only to learn he was out of town. He dialed a second man and a substitute secretary said the second man was away that day.

Said the chairman: "This is Gerstenberg. I want such-and-such a paper. Send it up to me." Then he hung up.

An associate sat in the office. Gerstenberg chuckled and said: "Now that girl isn't sure it was Gerstenberg on the line. She's inclined to think it was a joke. But she can't be sure—so she'll get the paper and send it up here. And then she'll say to some other girl—'wonder what Gerstenberg will think when he gets that piece of paper he doesn't know anything about.'"

Hobson's Choice

A magazine writer came to Detroit during a period when relationships between the CIO United Auto Workers Union and the various companies were under severe strain. This writer sought out Lou Seaton of General Motors, sat down, and started the conversation with a blunt question: "What do you think of Walter Reuther?"

The labor relations expert came right back. "I have four opinions of Walter Reuther. You'll get the official one."

And that was all he got.

Wilsonians

Shortly after World War II the Fisher brothers left active management posts in General Motors, and a rumor went around that they were going to buy the Oldsmobile division and operate it themselves. One day the man then the business editor of The Detroit Times, Ward Schultz, and I talked about this in the GM Building lobby.

"We ought to get more out of this story than a 'no comment'," we agreed. We went up to General Motors public relations and told our story to the only man there, Tom Rhoades, "Will you carry a message up to Mr. Wilson?" we asked.

"Sure," he said. "Why not?"

He returned shortly with a semi-dazed look in his eyes. "Mr. Wilson will see you right away," he said.

We rode up to the 14th floor and went in to the president's office. He demolished the Fisher-Olds story in a few minutes. At that point, we were seated and at ease and had a fine opportunity to interview—so we did. Thirty minutes went by as we talked about various matters of concern, and then we started to leave.

Wilson accompanied us to the door. He shook hands with Schultz, then with Rhoades, then with me, and we walked out. Obviously Wilson wasn't sure which of the three of us was his publicist.

"Well," said Rhoades. "You see how often I get up here!"

Wilson often stayed overnight in the ascetic and plain bedrooms maintained for executives on the top floor of the General Motors building in Detroit. His fellow executives enjoyed him and his observations, but they were apt to groan inwardly when he approached any of them around 6 p.m., when they customarily left for the day. If he leaned on the sill of an office door and began to talk in leisurely fashion, they were fairly sure that he was staying in the building overnight—and hence had nothing to do except eat before he retired between 9 and 10 p.m. Having time to pass and much on his mind, he would stand and engage in conversation for an hour or two or even longer, while his unwilling vice-presidential subordinate kept up his end of the conversation—and wondered how he would be received when he arrived home hours late for dinner!

Just before Wilson was picked by President-elect Eisenhower to become Secretary of Defense, he ran into Harry Coen, vice president in charge of employee communications at General Motors, and the two of them noted that the following February 1, less than two months away, Coen would retire.

Said Coen: "I don't think I could do anything, C.E., that would cause you to fire me before February 1."

Wilson meditated a while. "Don't work too hard at it, Harry," he said.

Epilogue

Robert Anderson, who went from a major engineering post at Chrysler to the presidency of Rockwell International, entertained some of his one-time Detroit press friends at dinner and recalled the days of lavish previews.

"People are still having fun," he said thoughtfully. "But—they're other people."